D0916576

Anyone who has had the pleasure of listening to Bert Lucarelli play and the thrill of talking to him about music and life will instantly hear his authentic voices in this book. Anyone who had yet to do either of those things will become eager at once to do if not both then either one or the other. This book is a great read either way and no one can come away with the experience unmoved by the intelligent artistic mind that brings together both the performance and the thoughtfulness that inevitably underpin music at its most transcending.

—Charles Middleton,
President (ret.), Middleton University

Daniel Pereira's conversations with Bert Lucarelli demonstrate how consciousness can be illuminated through the arts. The rituals and rhythms of this remarkable performer's life provide insights into in ways in which engaging with music, and all humanities, allows us to flourish fully as human beings.

—Lynn Pasquerella,
President, Mt. Holyoke College

It's not easy to pick out the oboist in a symphony orchestra, but you certainly can hear the solos. Similarly, you can find a lot of musicians offering snapshot comments during PBS interviews, without really knowing what makes them tick, what they actually think about conductors, how they learn a new score, how they teach an old one. In his long and wonderfully productive career, Bert Lucarelli has seen, done and remembered it all, and via this fascinating set of conversations, we get to learn it all. I've shared a number of delectable broadcast hours with Bert; now it's your turn to share his sparkling wit and musical magic.

—Robert Sherman, WQXR

Not only is Bert Lucarelli one of America's greatest musicians but he's also a legendary raconteur. We Can't Always Play Waltzes is therefore as illuminating and insightful as it is tremendous fun to read. In short, it's clearly the work of that rarest of musicians: a man who talks music every bit as thrillingly as he plays it.

—Jim Svejda, KUSC

We Can't Always Play Waltzes
CONVERSATIONS WITH BERT LUCARELLI

Bert

Lucarelli

We Can't Always Play Waltzes
CONVERSATIONS WITH BERT LUCARELLI

by DANIEL PEREIRA
Foreword by HENRY FOGEL
Edited by NICHOLAS HOPKINS

Photo by Michael Fiedler

Printed in Canada
ISBN 978-0-8258-8829-8

Carl Fischer is a privately owned music publisher founded in 1872.

CEO: Sonya Kim
Senior Graphic Designer: Andy Dowty
Managing Editor: Nicholas Hopkins

Carl Fischer, LLC
www.carlfischer.com

Table of Contents

The New York Times

MONDAY, NOVEMBER 16, 1970

*

Lucarelli, Oboist, Is a Lyric Delight

Bert Lucarelli is a first-rate oboist, and his enthusiasm for the instrument and its solo literature has led him to schedule three appearances at Tully Hall this season. Whether his expectations of public response to justify all of them will be realized remains to be seen. In any case, the first event, given Saturday night, was a delight from beginning to end.

Under the heading "The Romantic Oboe," Mr. Lucarelli offered works for oboe and piano by Schumann, Barthe, Saint-Säens, Nielsen and Poulenc and Reinecke's Trio for oboe, French horn and piano.

It was a program in which lyricism predominated, and Mr. Lucarelli's playing had the smoothness and songfulness of a beautiful voice perfectly produced

Since the performances of Martin Katz, the pianist, and Howard Howard, the French-horn player, equaled Mr. Lucarelli's in precision and sensitivity, the evening was one of total musical pleasure.

ALLEN HUGHES.

Foreword

Memoirs of performing artists seem to follow a fairly predictable structure. They typically begin with a recounting of the genesis of a musical career, followed by a list of triumphant professional performance highlights, and sprinkled along the way with some amusing tidbits of not-too-candid backstage gossip. But actual insights into the art of music or the act of performing are rarely offered. Serious introspection and critical self-analysis seem to be foreign to memoirs.

Such is not the case here. Humbert Lucarelli, one of the rare classical musicians (and perhaps the only American one) who enjoy a successful career as a solo oboist, has engaged in very serious (but not humorless) conversation with Daniel Pereira. This is extraordinary because it offers a window into the music and philosophy of one of America's most important musicians. The probing, knowledgeable questions asked by Dr. González play a major role in drawing out Bert's most deep and intimate musical thoughts.

 One special attribute of this set of "conversations" is they offer genuine meaning and value to both casual and knowledgeable music lovers alike, as well as to the professional musician, a bridge not that easy to build. The relaxed and interpersonal tone of this memoir makes for easy reading; one can almost hear the voices of both participants even if one has never heard them speak. This very human and warm tone offers the reader a privileged look into Bert's very special world.

One of the things that has always frustrated me with many of those who write about music is their oftentimes black-and-white approach to what is said about the art. "This is the right way to perform this piece," or "Mozart is without question the greatest composer," or "No, Beethoven is the greatest composer," or Bach is, or whomever. Bert's insistence on the complexity of the art and his own refusal to take black-and-white stands is a wonderfully refreshing thread that runs throughout these exchanges. His use of phrases like "Let me contradict myself," or "You see that I am conflicted," contrast strikingly with those writers whose absolute opinions are encased in cement, and for whom differing opinions seem to exist as an opportunity for ridicule.

Many of Bert's interchanges with Daniel Pereira (who is a distinguished pianist, scholar and pedagogue) are of a deeply personal nature. Music lovers will not only enjoy, but also will learn from, Bert's recollections of rehearsing and working with great conductors and musicians such as Stokowski, Solti, Krips, Reiner, Kondrashin, and Stravinsky. Bert entices us into his world with many insightful observations.

The reader will also gain candid insights into Bert's personality. When asked how he chose to pursue a solo career, Bert explains he rented Carnegie Recital Hall, using funds from a grant of the Rockefeller Foundation. His performance was reviewed by Howard Klein, music critic of the *New York Times*, who wrote: "Bert Lucarelli is a consummate oboe player and could play at any major orchestra in the country, but the oboe is not a solo instrument." Bert's response is beautifully revealing: "Well, that was a problem for me, because don't ever tell me no. Never, never, never tell me no."

What is revealed in page after page of these conversations is someone who, beyond being a great musician, is also a great humanist—someone who thinks about the world and the people in it, and the place of the arts in our lives. What also comes across are insights into performing that will be instructive to other performers, but also informative to music lovers, as it will allow them greater insight into what it takes for that person on the stage to be making music for those of us in the audience. There are serious thoughts here about the essence of music, and of musical analysis, that are expressed in language that the layman can comprehend (no need to be a musicologist here). And there is great candor.

One of the most valuable and engaging chapters is Chapter 5, The Proust Questionnaire. It was a list of questions popular in the late nineteenth century, a list that Proust completed while a teenager, and is designed to give insight into the personality of the respondent. Dr. González posed these questions to Bert, who answered them candidly and willingly. I think my favorite answer was to the question "What is your favorite virtue?" Bert replies: "Generosity of spirit. By that I mean one of not condemning. A willingness, even eagerness, to accept others and the ideas of others."

That answer sums up the tone of this entire set of exchanges. Bert's openness to the ideas, thoughts, and the musical imaginations of others, plus his willingness through a long career to consistently re-think his own musical ideas, is both refreshing and elucidating. I found, in reading through these, I was challenged to re-examine some of my own long-held beliefs, and from that, I learned a great deal. Daniel Barenboim, Music Director of the Chicago Symphony, with whom I had the privilege of working for many years, was fond of saying, "The greatest musicians are those who feel with their brain and think with their heart." That has always been a statement I have treasured, and it is clear from these conversations that Bert Lucarelli is such a musician.

It is most rare for an artist's reminiscences to be as provocative, stimulating, and even intellectually challenging as these. I hope they will be as enlightening and illuminating to the reader as they are for me.

—Henry Fogel
Dean, Chicago College of Performing Arts, Roosevelt University
Former President, Chicago Symphony Orchestra and
League of American Orchestras

Acknowledgements

These conversations would not have seen public light without the invaluable assistance of the following colleagues and friends, who very kindly contributed their time and expertise to help.

My sincerest gratitude goes to all: Cynthia Cannell, Gerald Carp, David Dutkanicz, Ellen Echeverria, Paula Frosch, Rose Ginsberg, Paul Hawkshaw, Bonnie Lichter, Sondra Myers, Sheldon Patinkin, Terry and Mary Stanton and Imanuel Willheim

And most especially thanks to Dr. Jan E. Holly for her painstaking editing of the original transcript.

A Brief Note to the Reader from Bert

Thanks to my mom who provided a platform of love and confidence that allows me to exist.

About five years ago I met Cynthia Cannell who is a literary agent. She encouraged me to write about my unusual experiences in my profession. When I got to about Chapter 5 I had to stop. It seemed too uncomfortable and self-aggrandizing to write about myself.

At that time I had a piano student from Spain, Daniel Pereira who needed help with developing musical ideas and expression so he suggested I give him some lessons, and offered to interview me to help break the block. What resulted was about twenty-three hours of conversation. This conversation has been written for young players pursuing a career in music and the general public who want to know something about performing.

Hoping it will be an inspiration to students and young entry-level performers as they travel the tough waters that will challenge them. It is precisely about what much of our life-work has been about.

It is a positive exploration of my adventure. Talking about some of the unusual things that have happen in my journey.

What follows, as the title states, is a conversation and as such is not in the form of a finely crafted smooth prose. Daniel and I decided that it would be better to leave it alone in all of its natural roughness and even occasionally with personal insights that are sometimes too close to the truth, especially in my impromptu responses to Daniel's thoughtful questions.

I certainly hope I have not offended anyone by the sin of omission or a misinterpretation of what resides in my memory.

14

Photo by Christian Steiner, 1970

Introduction

The Open Night was a television show, broadcast on Spanish Public Television in the late 1990s, hosted by a controversial personage named Pedro Ruiz, whom I greatly admired. Every Thursday night, and during six seasons, the program was televised on the channel known as "The Second." In the course of the sixty minutes of the production, Pedro Ruiz would interview a personality of interest in a rather unconventional, intimate and candid manner. On the other side of the screen, there was I, enthralled by the captivating and attractive exchange between the questioner and the interviewee.

Since then, I have been truly fascinated by this style of discussion and felt inclined to undertake a similar venture of my own. Learning and discovering what respected intellectuals, politicians, entertainers and artists have to say, have always appealed to me enormously.

Humbert Lucarelli has always been an artist and pedagogue of genuine interest to me, since I met him at the University of Hartford (Connecticut) in 2002. Years later, in the early fall of 2010, having had many engaging conversations with maestro Lucarelli, the idea of interviewing him emerged. In spite of the fact that Lucarelli reacted rather with resistance to my proposal, he agreed to get the ball rolling shortly after. It was in December of that year, that the *conversations*, as we resolved to call them, excitingly kicked off.

For the following two years, Bert (a nickname that will be used from now on) and I conducted a series of riveting talks, either in person or via the Internet. These unforgettable talks will remain amongst the most gratifying moments of my life. The spontaneity, sagacity and depth of Bert's reflections facilitated the progress of the project and provided countless hours of enjoyment and learning.

These conversations would have not come to fruition without the immensely valuable contribution of Dr. Jan E. Holly, to whom I am deeply grateful for her witty and joyous suggestions. I must also thank Rose Ginsberg who, painstakingly and masterfully, transcribed all the audio recordings and graciously managed my inborn Spanish accent with no problem.

My sincerest gratitude goes to Henry Fogel, former president of the Chicago Symphony Orchestra and currently the Dean of the Chicago College of Performing Arts, Roosevelt University, who kindly wrote the generous foreword for this book.

A number of footnotes have been added, when they were considered necessary for the better comprehension of the text or simply to add some light to certain aspects of the talks.

I can only hope that these conversations will engender as much joy in the readers as they did to me. Why can't we always play waltzes? Turn the page to find out!

—Daniel Pereira
Fairfax, Virginia September 2014

Chapter One: Arts in Our Life

Daniel Pereira: *Bert, I think the readers might be wondering, why can't we always play waltzes?*

Humbert Lucarelli: The title We Can't Always Play Waltzes comes from an impromptu conversation that a friend and I had in Chicago. Her name is Joan Bennett. She was a flutist in The Chicago Symphony Orchestra. I played with her at Grant Park in Chicago, which is a large concert series free to the public. She played principal flute and, I played principal oboe. One morning, at a rehearsal, she said to me, "I just had the most amazing experience. Coming down the elevator from my apartment, there was an older Viennese woman who got in the elevator with me. She saw the flute under my arm and said, 'Oh my, are you the flutist who I hear?'" And, embarrassed, Joan told me she said to her, "I hope you don't mind that I play scales and exercises every morning." And the woman replied, "That is fine my dear. We can't always play waltzes."

I always thought that this was a very philosophical concept about life. We can't always be happy and do what we like. Sometimes, we have to work and embrace all of those things that will make us better; that there is a flip side (maybe a dark side) to whatever we think is success.

How do you define the role of the arts and the artists in society?

Ah, a two-part question. My thinking is hardly original: The arts help us to go inside—to the interior—to understand our emotions, and even to explore the very concept of our feelings. We are too often afraid of our feelings, because they are often complex and difficult. We prefer to avoid talking about them. Art allows us to be a bit more objective about our own feelings. It is an experience upon which we can project our emotion, and it even helps us to become aware of emotions that we may never even knew we had.

So, as I speak, I analyze my ideas a little bit—going on a tangent in my mind. The whole notion of being moved fascinates me. First, it is about music. The listener hears a piece of music and the entire body, literally, wants to move. It's a visceral reaction. The same occurs with painting. The exquisite lines of a Picasso compel me, internally, to sway from side to side. Most challenging is literature; to move a reader with language.

Of course, you know the saying, "Art is in the eye of the beholder." Now we go into the sphere of the audience and the performer, the artist. For the artist, art is pretty much the act of communication. But communication implies both that the artist has something to say and that the listener wishes to hear or feel it. The artist's obligation is to find that connection.

Is art selective or an activity available to only a few? Is it elitist?

No. No, no, no, no, no. Every individual has the potential to engage with the arts. It's not elite, but the desire and willingness to take that journey into artistic experience is personal and essential. Witnessing individuals, who appear to care little about art and later discover that they can profoundly express feelings that are reflected in art, touches me because the experience can be deeply personal.

Recently, I had dinner with a relative who prefers to believe that he holds no strong feelings. He is always bantering and joking, but listening carefully and asking non-threatening important questions—without overwhelming him—elicited from him the most provocative and profound insights. It was stunning.

Do all human beings have a predisposition to understand art—to understand music—and to be affected by it?

Yes, yes, yes. Now we begin, by defining our terms. By "understand," do we mean comprehending the harmonic progression, knowing what key we are in? Taking in the sensation? Recognizing where the music is headed? Understanding it mentally, physically or intellectually?

The term "understand" is not up to the task of explaining the impact of art. Nor should we believe that appreciation requires "understanding." At an art venue, like the Metropolitan Museum of Art in New York City, I can look at a painting, be quite taken by it yet remain oblivious of the techniques that created it. I am not convinced that "intellectual understanding" of art increases depth of appreciation. It is a different kind of understanding.

On the other hand, let me argue against myself. Typically, I am uncomfortable with opera productions that project the translated libretto onto a screen for audiences to read during the performance. Reading interferes with the listening experience. On the other hand, knowing the words a little bit helps me comprehend, for example, that a performer colors while singing a vowel—"ooh"—may add some dramatic meaning and depth that may be associated with that specific sound. Bright vowels may mean something else: excitement. They may signify happiness or cheer. I can't reconcile this completely in my own head.

Then again, I am reminded of my experience at the French National Theatre in New York, seeing plays presented entirely in French. Although the language was incomprehensible to me, I could follow the action. I failed to pick up on some of the subtleties but I knew what was happening.

Language can interfere with communication as much as it can help. A great composer and also a great performer can help bridge that gap.

I am reminded of an article in Lewis Lapham's quarterly *Means of Communication* (Spring 2012), in which he presents an article by Denis Diderot who was a prominent eighteenth-century French philosopher, art critic and writer discussing the complex relationship of musical sound, color and the language of words. Diderot was an influential philosopher during the Enlightenment, and is best known for serving as co-founder, chief editor and contributor to the *Encyclopédie*. He said he often put his fingers in his ears when watching plays performed, that the visual could be more penetrating than the words. In this regard Lapham also quotes Marcel Marceau saying in 1958, "Do not the most moving moments of our lives find us all without words?"

So, you are not an advocate of programmatic music? Does abstract music appeal to you more?

It need not be one or the other. Art exists only in relation to itself. I was taught that Beethoven's "Emperor" Concerto was not written for the emperor. The publisher added the title, as a marketing ploy, to sell the music. Likewise, the "Eroica" Symphony. Such pieces were composed in the abstract. But, let me contradict myself. If art is an act of communication, it communicates viscerally and fundamentally. It does not need a literal description and so the audience can participate in that creative experience.

Contemporary composers who give their pieces dramatic titles, like "The Hiroshima Catastrophe," annoy me. I want to decide whether the music has value on its own merit. The marketing title interferes with my feelings about the music. I do not need to be nudged into believing that a piece of music is important because it is about Hiroshima or the dropping of the bomb.

But this would apply less to opera or Lieder, I assume, because opera depends on a story, correct?

Yes, exactly. You see that I am conflicted. I have no simple answer. We talked once about Bernstein's Norton lectures,[1] and his exploration of language's influence on music. Such an incredibly important subject! Language is important to music, not only because it affects the meaning, but as vowel sounds affect the line, and the rhythm. You know, I just did it: "And the rhythm." "Ba-da-bi-do." Musicians routinely argue about whether the words or the notes are more important, or which came first. My response is that it varies, from phrase to phrase and perhaps from note to note. These questions composers think about and talk about, but not the audience who experiences the composition on a different level.

Wait, wait. Perhaps a performer should know. When you practice, do you not attempt to understand the motivation behind the rhythm and behind the harmony?

I personally cannot take a fixed position on this. I argue about it with friends who believe that knowing exactly which word is sung at which moment is crucial. But in the end, if the composer did his job, and the performers do their job, then the listener gets the message. Am I wrong? The meaning should be there. It should stand on its own. We don't need a libretto or verbal guide for every note of music

But what is a work of art? A work of art exists in relationship to itself, not necessarily to an event or a specific subject. For example, opera. Plots of tragic operas are so often absurd, almost comical. Although Gluck's *Orfeo* is deep and serious in terms of its suggestion of what is a universal theme, the plot and setting are ridiculous. But you don't laugh at the plot. You are moved by your empathetic feeling for the characters. Am I making a decent point here?

1   A series of six lectures at Harvard University, titled *The Unanswered Question*, presented in 1973 by Leonard Bernstein.

Can we go back to the role of the artist in society and particularly to the role of the musician? Should we all practice making art, professionals and non-professionals alike? Should everyone try to make music or paint or write poetry?

Yes. I admire those who are not professionals, but rather aficionados of art. It matters little whether the medium is music or painting or writing or whatever. Regardless, it puts the individual in contact with the possibility of expressing what she or he really feels or wishes to say. To me, that is art: the expression of an interior feeling.

For the performer so much of it is the desire to share: to share a moment or to share something special, something personal. To succeed the artist must go inside and determine: What does this mean to me? What am I feeling? What am I doing? That is the first step; before I can share something, I must first clarify its meaning to myself.

Anyone engaged in this kind of endeavor has my admiration. I met recently with a man who taught negotiation at Harvard. Most fascinating was hearing him discuss his skill at discovering what the other person, the receptor, was capable of receiving. He was trained to do this, which is a difficult, but important skill for a performer to acquire. Oh, you remember Horowitz, who posed the question of why do people come to a concert. One group comes to be seen. Another comes to enjoy the performer and the performance. A last group comes to hear the mistakes, what you do wrong. So, as a performer, you play to a varied audience. Focusing on any one of the groups is a terrible mistake. Focusing only on those who are present to have a good time and be moved by you is also not good enough.

For example, I taught a class at The Hartt School called "The Business of Music." It was dedicated to helping students determine what to do after graduation. The class didn't work for me because the constituency was so varied, so broad. Some were oboe players who wanted orchestral positions. Pianists wanted to play in dance studios. Others wanted church jobs playing organ. Instrumentalists wanted solo careers. Well, how to talk to all those aspiring musicians with a single idea? I couldn't; I couldn't find one subject that would engage all of them, with the exception of the concept of bringing quality to whatever they do, and as a musician how to do your taxes.

So, in a concert you have a little bit of that because certainly. It's like fishing with a net. You throw the net over the audience, and pull them in. You hope that enough of them in the audience will relate to what you are doing. I can only feel positive; It doesn't work for me to feel negative.

Since we are talking about concerts, I have the impression that not everyone can be moved by a Mahler symphony, a Beethoven sonata or Schubert Lieder. So here we come to the conflict between popular music and classical music. Is classical music really only for an exclusive few? Not necessarily because people don't have access to classical music, but because popular music speaks in a more direct language for a much larger population.

Well, about popular music, it is difficult to generalize because even the songs of Gershwin, Rodgers, Kern, Porter, that whole crowd, are now considered by many to be American art songs. The principal motivation of popular music is to sell, to make money, to grab the audience. For art music or classical music, the motivation is a little more complex. The classical artist wants to relate to something universal, something that goes very, very deep that is beyond personal. Consequently, it out of necessity has a greater variety. It's so easy to look down our noses at popular music because it addresses a much larger audience. Mistake. Certainly popular artists also try to reach for the deeply personal, maybe in a simpler and more direct fashion. You just can't generalize. Can you think of anything much deeper than John Lennon's Imagine?

But many classical composers—for instance, Beethoven—did just that: selling music to make a living.

Sure. Bach was probably the most commercial composer of all time. He wrote a cantata every week. It's like he was writing for a television series. We elevate Bach, place him on a pedestal; but in the end, he wrote for the most commercial institution of his time. The church was the television of its day. It was trying to bring people out of their houses, and into the church. And artists were the means to help accomplish that task. Musicians had to write music—dramatic, moving music—to persuade people to come.

The church—I don't know whether it is fair to say only "the church," but let's use it for the moment—has often used the arts to draw people into its doors. People come to hear their friends perform and to sit with the artwork, the paintings and sculptures; all of that art is designed to bring us in.

So a conflict exists between the act of choosing a program based not only on what I would like to perform, but what I hope the audience will want to hear, or the presenter will want to present. One recording I made was of American music. The program was chosen because I was applying for a grant from the National Endowment for the Arts, and I knew what the adjudicators wanted. They wanted to promote American music. So, I found the repertoire that would persuade them to fund my project. What's the option? Choose a repertoire that will not result in funding? Forget about it; it is a futile exercise.

There's nothing wrong with reaching out to your audience. Sometimes I joke about contemporary composers and presenters who say they don't care if the audience comes, or not. They are not writing for the audience. In that case I don't go. I never go to a party to which I have not been invited. But in the end I always chose music to listen to and perform that I like or challenges me, valuable music that, in my opinion, deserves to be heard. So, even within the restriction, I put a program together that satisfied both the National Endowment and myself. Sometimes artists function best within clearly defined parameters. A composer writes best if he has a particular "box" within which to work, like a symphonic form. Some of the best music is written for films. Some of the worst art is the results from self-indulgence.

This discussion is reminding me of a dinner party I went to in Chicago that had an impressive list of well-known guests. At one point I was talking with a nice man who told me he was an architect. He was fascinated with the idea that I was a musician. So I explained to him that as a young person I was more interested in becoming an architect. In fact, I had done architectural drawings of buildings that I thought would be different. I told him that one of the stupidest drawings I did was of an apartment building that was round, but had to get it on to paper and out of my system. It was a circular or round building with the entry to each apartment in the center of the building so that when you entered the apartment it was at its smallest and the further you went in to the apartment it became larger. The result being that the biggest part of the apartment was the outdoor terrace. I said to him, "Obviously, a dumb idea."

"Really," he said, "I had the same idea and talked them into building it!" "Oh no," I said, "you're Bertrand Goldberg, the architect of Marina Towers in Chicago." He laughed and encouraged me to laugh, too, but it was difficult with my foot in my mouth.

We later corresponded about the relationship of music and architecture. He was giving a lecture on the subject for The Chicago Symphony, and he thought our conversation helpful.

Do you think that so much experimentation in twentieth-century music was positive? Bach experimented, as did Haydn, Mozart and Beethoven.

Yes. Composers or architects for that matter can't just do what is being done. They must test new ideas, that reflect and challenge the environment, past, present and future. But, but just being aggressive about being different is a waste of time. It's important to keep a balance

Did the extreme avant-garde of the twentieth century injure contemporary classical music?

Extremism spoils; it's too narrow. It has its place, but retaining a historical perspective is essential. For me, the most remembered and respected composers of history are those who were not so much experimental, but who brought together all that could be said within the particular context that came before. Bach completed the baroque period. Composers were unable to engage with baroque music after Bach, because he had basically said it all. So we entered into a kind of corruption of baroque music into the rococo.

Mozart ended the classical period. Also, Haydn and Beethoven. They concluded the language of their period, and effected a transition to another. The Ninth Symphony is, in some regard, romantic; the recitative in the last movement is a very dramatic moment. It fascinates me that The Beatles seem to have had the last say about popular music.

Yes, the Ninth Symphony is absolutely romantic.

But it starts out classical. And as I mentioned earlier, the "Eroica » did not have that romantic title. The publisher added it, like in Beethoven's fifth piano concerto, nicknamed the "Emperor."

In Beethoven's manuscript of the "Eroica" symphony, the inscription that was originally intended for the so-called "heroic" Napoleon was later re-dedicated to a "fallen hero."

Great, now here you're teaching me something. Never-the-less the concept of "heroic" can be an abstraction, don't you think? It is unspecific. Which is not to say that the act of writing, or creating, an abstraction doesn't contain some interior emotional component. Even a completely abstract painting can provoke a visceral response.

So, does enjoying music depend exclusively on feeling or do you think that the more musical and technical understanding we have, the better we appreciate it?

Classical music is like an onion. It has many layers. You can come to it in any way you like.

But is it just about feelings, about listening to a piece of music to feel something, or does knowledge and education enhance the experience? Can we appreciate better a Bach fugue when we understand the fugue, how it works and the operation of its technical devices?

Certainly, it is more than just feelings. Feeling is only one path. When you hear a fugue, you hear the theme's statement. And then another statement comes. So, knowing that the second statement is coming, does it distract, or is it better to have that prior knowledge? Or if you just listen to it naively, and then you are moved by the fact that it is becoming more complex, or does it draw you in? Is that better or worse? You are alluding to the importance of understanding the craft. To understand the craft is not so important for a general audience. In fact if we insist on it, it may intimidate them and unnecessarily turn them away for no reason. Just let them enjoy it. Later if they want to know more, they can.

Anthony Tommasini, the New York Times chief music critic, published a list of the top-ten composers of all time, except for those who are still alive. Johann Sebastian Bach was at the top of the list. This may or may not be a surprise. Baroque music, particularly Bach's music, is very complex, sophisticated and intricate. His expressive language is not so uncomplicated as Schubert Lieder or a Mozart melody.

Wasn't Schubert also very near the top of that list? Listening to the music of Bach and feeling its complexity puts us in touch with our own complexity, and that can be very moving, even if we do not talk about it. One of my favorite musical moments is the opening of the Saint Matthew Passion. I love it so much because it is complex while projecting a simple feeling of the eternal. Hearing it makes me feel that it will go on forever, and that it is forever.

I am reminded of James Joyce's writing about eternity, when he compares the years in eternity to grains of sand on the beaches of the world. That is the same feeling I get in the opening of the *Saint Matthew Passion.* But I don't "understand" it according to the traditional meaning of that word. I understand it on a subliminal, visceral level. It is the fourth *canto.*[2] I *appreciate* it—wouldn't that be a better word, to say appreciate, rather than understand? I mean this not in a sense of liking it, but to appreciate it with the generosity of acceptance.

Understanding comes in several forms. It can be an intellectual, emotional, physical or spiritual knowing. Any one of these forms taking over completely will make a distortion.

I have Tommasini's list in front of me. Of course it is a subjective list because he asked only a handful of readers. But it is still remarkable. It comes out to this: No. 1, J. S. Bach; No. 2, Beethoven; No. 3, Mozart; No. 4, Schubert; No. 5, Debussy; No. 6, Stravinsky; No. 7, Brahms; No. 8, Verdi; No. 9, Wagner; and No. 10, Bartók. It seems a controversial list. What do you think about it?

It is subjective, very subjective. Some people scoff at the idea of doing a list like this. I love such lists, because they make us think. Would you have ordered it differently? I forget Tommasini's explanation for placing Schubert so high on the list. But I can appreciate it. Ah, I just substituted "appreciate" for "understand." I can appreciate it, because Schubert's music speaks directly, with a simplicity that is pure. It has the illusion of being so naïve. Its innocence makes you cry. It is uncomplicated. We make the mistake of wanting it to be complicated. We often believe art to be more profound if it is more complex.

My teacher, Robert Bloom said to me once, "Oboe playing is not so complicated, it's just difficult." Again, it made me think about life.

Yes, making such a list is dangerous. The point of the list is to pose the question: What music speaks most directly to the largest number of people? It could be Beethoven, or Schubert, or Brahms, or...

...is Schumann in this picture?

No. Neither is Mendelssohn; Mahler isn't either nor is Haydn or Strauss. Not even Tchaikovsky, who is beloved by many, including myself.

Tommasini said that when he goes to sleep at night he fears that the many great composers whom we love, who were not on the list, will come into to his dreams, his nightmares and haunt him. Did Tommasini not say that he wished the list numbered at least 100?

---

2   Canto is a principal form of division in a long poem.

But still, it's not about the number, but about…

The act. It took courage for Tommasini to do that list.

And the order. In the process, you are forced to assign numbers.

Recently, at an Academy Awards ceremony, one of the winners said, "You know, what is really disappointing about all of this is it is about who is best. In art, there is no best." I love that. It is so true.

In the classical-music world today there are a large number of orchestras, but many of them are near bankruptcy or operating with large deficits. Smaller communities support orchestras, even some community colleges have orchestras. But do we really need so many orchestras, given the fact that society seems incapable of supporting them? What do you think is happening?

Ah, one of my favorite subjects. Concerts are not only ticket-driven. We should have as many orchestras as the public will come to. Support is not only financial; attending is the most important support. The number of paying customers does not drive the art. Art is driven by sponsorship as well, and the desire to be enlightened and have a good time. It always has been. Not even sports events are solely ticket driven. Allow me to make a broad statement and say that the act of performance is not ticket driven.

To understand the concert more clearly, we need to return to the Renaissance. As we were talking earlier, in the Renaissance, the church brought music from outdoors, from the fields, where people staged celebrations and festivals and the church brought these events into a building, into a space. Music was brought indoors and as I mentioned before was used to bring people into the church.

At the same time, music was made in the home, in small rooms, with such instruments as the virginal, recorders, and with singers who sang with a small sound and no vibrato. Almost like the cabaret singers of today. As concerts moved into larger spaces they required serious sponsorship. The church did it at first. Broadly speaking, after the church, the aristocracy took over. That's what Becket's story is about, the competition between the church and the aristocracy.[3] When the aristocracy won, they took the responsibility. Another example of how winning brings responsibility. Sponsorship of all those institutions tells us who we are. After the aristocracy came the industrial revolution, with corporations taking responsibility. Is it possible that the profit-and-loss mindset of the corporate world is not the best for concerts? Is it possible that the beginning of popular music was really the industrial revolution, the building of the middle class?

I would like to ask you a question that has direct political implications. Under which presidential mandate or political party have the arts, particularly music, been most nourished or developed?

In my lifetime, it was the Kennedy years, of course. That was a dream, the Camelot years. The disappointment that many of us feel now is that

---

3   A 1964 British-American film adapted from the play *Becket or the Honor of God* by Jean Anouilh.

the Camelot did not continue. The Kennedy years produced a sense of responsibility about the future of the arts. The Kennedy Center is an important institution as is Lincoln Center. We dreamt at that time of a world that would be filled with art.

By art, I don't mean only so-called "high" art. I mean being comfortable with what you're doing and being sensitive to it, not just assuming. So, those were fantastic years, but the dream was left unrealized. Those of us who lived through those years seem disappointed that such positive times for the arts did not continue.

It's not so bad though. Think of the number of opera houses and concert halls as well as museums that have been built in the past twenty years and number of concerts that have increased. I remember when I was in my 20s and 30s there were so few concerts and summer festivals. Now they are all over the place competing with one another for audiences. There were only a few orchestras that had summer seasons. Now an orchestra is not considered a major orchestra if it does not have a full year-long season. We have grown, and we will continue.

Art is important because it encourages you to look within. During the Kennedy years artists were brought forward as being compelling and affecting change.

You may know my political bent; that I am pretty much a liberal or at least left of center. But the label "liberal" has been distorted. It has taken on a pejorative connotation; it's been demonized. When I was young, liberal meant being free, free to give, free to share, free from fear that you would not have enough for yourself, freedom in knowing that you do not need to be selfish or hold things only for yourself. This freedom to give comes from a fundamental sense of security in which you can give of yourself and not suffer. I love the word "liberal."

Chapter 2. Working under Celebrated Batons

Bert and Ascher Tempkin, Conductor after Mozart
Concerto, 1969

Daniel Pereira: *I would like to ask you about a few musicians with whom you have worked during your career. Shall we start with Igor Stravinsky?*

Humbert Lucarelli: Oh, of course! My love for Stravinsky goes back to my high-school days, when I wrote a term paper for an English class. The paper was about the life and career of Igor Stravinsky. I never imagined that I would play in an orchestra he was conducting in Carnegie Hall.

I was very impressed with Stravinsky, especially when I was a player in an orchestra that he was conducting. But because I was working with him, developing a detailed notion of him was not at the front of my mind. He was kind, gentle, and appreciative. If he didn't like something, he would say only, "No, no, try this. Do it this way." He was never intimidating or unreceptive.

There was one particular rehearsal that will remain with me forever. We were rehearsing the *Symphony of Psalms* and in the middle of the big oboe solo, in what I believe is the opening of the second movement, Stravinsky stopped and said to me, "Mr. Oboe, it's too musical." Of course, the whole orchestra laughed, and after a moment I realized what he meant. I was phrasing it with what I jokingly call my usual "macaronic Italian-opera style," and he wanted a more angular, mechanical approach. One should not forget that Stravinsky was part of the "man-against-machine" aesthetic of the early 1900s, just coming out of the shock of trying to absorb the industrial revolution. In my opinion, this concept starts with Charlie Chaplin's *Modern Times* and goes into Stanley Kubrick's *2001: A Space Odyssey*.

Robert Craft, who was Stravinsky's assistant, was incredibly kind to me. He led many of the preparation rehearsals for the concerts and recordings that Stravinsky conducted in which I participated. A musician of great accomplishment, Craft had extraordinary control of the orchestra.

I will never forget being in the orchestra for Stravinsky's last performances as a conductor. Among the works we performed was *Pulcinella* with that glorious second movement, a sarabande that is titled "Serenata" with its famous oboe solo that is now even used in orchestra auditions. In five performances, the tempo was radically different every night, from being in twelve beats to the measure to four beats. So much for finding the exact tempo the composer wants.

I recently heard a story about Stravinsky that illustrates his congeniality. He was late for a rehearsal that was being held for a recording of *L'Histoire du soldat* [4] that does not have oboes. so I wasn't there. The story goes that it was on a Sunday night, at about 11 p.m., the group was called together, and Stravinsky went directly to the studio from the airport, bringing along a bottle of Scotch. Before they started, he opened the bottle, took a big swig. Then, passing the bottle around to the players, he said, "I think we all have to have a good swallow of Scotch before we get started."

What about Leonard Bernstein?

I performed with Maestro Bernstein only once and was very impressed by his kindness and generosity. He also enjoyed having a good time. I played a solo at a rehearsal, and I am glad to say, he liked it and complimented me. Then, during the concert—it was in a big church, the Cathedral of Saint John the Divine,[5] which can be chilly—water condensed in my oboe in the middle of my solo and one of the notes started to bubble. Bernstein looked at me and laughed—not at all upset. Afterward, backstage, I went to see him said to him, "Maestro, I feel so sad and terrible that this happened." "Oh," he said, "are you kidding? These things always happen at concerts during solos!" He completely understood.

I frequently saw him in rehearsals where I was only an observer, not a player. The natural physical outpouring of his talent was particularly impressive. Many believed his expressive nature to be too overt, that it got in the way, that his so-called flamboyance was intended for the cameras or the audience. Not true. He was the same in rehearsals, very expressive and ebullient. Obviously, he doesn't need my acclamation. He was a magnificent musician and artist.

Can you also tell me about your experience with Kirill Kondrashin? [6]

He was such a beautiful person. His spirit and soul were absolutely incredible. He was at peace with himself. He had a major career in Russia during the years of the Iron Curtain that separated the West from Soviet Russia; a repressive government, and he just dealt with it. Kondrashin happened to be in the United States, in New York, to conduct the Van Cliburn Carnegie Hall concerts, immediately after Cliburn won the Tchaikovsky Competition that were conducted in Moscow by Kondrashin.[7]

---

4   *L'Histoire du soldat* (The Soldier's Tale) is a theatrical work by Igor Stravinsky, which includes reading, playing and dancing.

5   Located in New York City.

6   Kirill Kondrashin (1914–1981), Russian conductor.

7   Held in Moscow, Russia in 1958.

The conductor who had been originally engaged to lead the performance of *Butterfly* at The Lyric in Chicago took sick. Maestro Kondrashin had recently conducted *Butterfly* in Moscow, so Maestro Kondrashin was called to Chicago. He came to Chicago to conduct Renata Tebaldi.[8] His appearance was an emergency substitution.

At the only rehearsal we had with him he took the tempo for Butterfly's entrance very slowly, I mean, excruciatingly slowly—which was, of course, very beautiful. But it was virtually impossible to sing. Tebaldi stopped mid-way through her performance in the rehearsal and said, "*Maestro, non si può...* Maestro, I can't." The memory still brings tears to my eyes, so tenderly did he treat her. In response, he said, "If Tebaldi can't do it, then the tempo is wrong." Rarely does a conductor react with such flexibility and grace today.

During these rehearsals, the thought occurred to me that Russian oboists in Moscow must have trouble getting reed-making cane and other supplies for the oboe. I had recently ordered 100 pieces of wonderful oboe cane from my favorite supplier in France. During a break in rehearsal, I gave him all of it and handed him the little bag of cane saying, "Just do me a favor. Put this in your shoes on your trip back to Moscow, and give it to your principal oboe player." He started to cry. That is the kind of person he was. Obviously, he was a great musician. But he was also a person of great power, beauty and empathy.

That is a fantastic story. Thank you very much for sharing it. What about Josef Krips? [9]

Josef Krips was one of the most self-assured human beings I have ever met in my life. I wish I could be as self-assured as he was. Krips was convinced that he knew what he was doing, and he knew what was always right. He made me principal oboist at the Lyric Opera of Chicago, after a specific incident, which occurred during a rehearsal of Mozart's Così fan tutte. The principal oboist at the time was just a terrific oboist, but she didn't quite have the necessary digital facility. Some of the oboe parts in Così's overture are technically very challenging. Krips kept pushing her and pressing her. It wasn't necessary. Finally, being so intimidated and humiliated, she broke down in tears and left the pit in the middle of the rehearsal. So, the Maestro asked me if I would move over and play principal for the remainder of the rehearsal.

I was a young punk who was sure, like Krips, that I could just do anything. So, I just went ahead and played it. I virtually sight-read the part. Not really sight-read it—I had studied it before, but not for any particular performance. So I played it. Krips stopped the orchestra and said, "This is a very strange orchestra. The second players play better than the first." This

---

8   Renata Tebaldi (1922–2004), Italian opera singer.

9   Josef Alois Krips (1902–1974), Austrian conductor and violinist.

statement embarrassed me. I asked the orchestra's contractor, "Is it okay for me to be doing this? What should I be doing?" He said, "Yes, just go ahead and play."

During a break in rehearsal, Krips went to the administrative office and told the managers, "Whenever I am conducting, that young man will be my principal oboe player." So there I was, a totally inexperienced principal oboist. I had some facility, but I had no idea what I was really doing. But I did it. He was generous to me. "Don't worry," he said, "I will show you everything. I even teach Schwarzkopf."[10] So, that was the extent of his ego: "I even teach Schwarzkopf." I mean, just a moment, please. Elisabeth Schwarzkopf was a monumental artist. Where did he get off saying that? I would love to know. Sometimes I wish I could think like him.

You have such vivid recollections of your life, and those recollections are so available to you. I ask you to recall something, and immediately the memories come tumbling out of your mind.

Well, if the memory is about a rehearsal, it could have happened this morning.

I'm embarrassed to tell you this story but think I have to.

Tullio Serafin was probably my most important influence during my early years of playing in terms of phrasing and color. He was loosely considered the chief of the post World War II international wing of Italian opera. Singers such as Callas, Sutherland and Tebaldi referred to him as their maestro. When I became principal in the Lyric Opera he conducted most of the Italian operas, He knew immediately that I was inexperienced but was eager to learn. During the break in most of the orchestra rehearsals he would come down from the podium sit next to me and show me what was coming next in the rehearsal. He warned me about difficult passages that were coming in the next hour and showed me what I might do to make a solo more beautiful, which notes to emphasize, which ones to play a little brighter or darker and so on.

When I went home at night after performances with him my dad would wait up and want to know the details what Serafin told me and of how the performances went. My father was a great fan of Italian Opera and knew very well who Tullio Serafin was. One night my dad asked me if he could meet the Maestro. So the next day during a rehearsal I told Maestro Serafin about my Dad and asked if it was okay to bring my father back stage to meet him. The Maestro said, of course bring my dad to his dressing room after a performance and two nights later after I got my dad a ticket for the performance I brought my father back stage to meet the Maestro.

I knocked on his dressing room door and he opened the door shirtless. He remembered immediately why I was there and invited my father and me into his dressing room. His wife was giving him a rubdown with alcohol. I can still remember the smell as if it was last night. I introduced them to each

---

10 Elisabeth Schwarzkopf (1915–2006), German-born soprano.

other and my father spoke to him in Italian and thanked him personally for everything he was doing for me. At that point the Maestro stopped my father and just said to him that some day his son was going to become a wonderful musician. I understood all of this because as the son of an immigrant, Italian was my first language. My father was a weeper and began to cry; next I started to cry. It was like a yawn or yawn virus that hit the room. Serafin's wife began to cry. Next the Maestro started to get tears in his eyes. It was like a ridiculous scene from a B-movie. My father being accustomed to the drama of Italian operas said to Serafin, "I give you my son!" This is all true. At that point thankfully someone knocked on the door—in fact, it was Byron Belt an assistant to Carol Fox who was the stunning Director of The Lyric Opera—my father collected himself we excused ourselves and left the dressing room.

I couldn't believe my father did that and didn't talk to him all the way on the drive home. I was embarrassed.

Were there any other conductors from the "Italian Post-World War II era" who influenced you?

Of course, I could never forget the impact the conductor Antonino Votto who had an effect on everything I felt about the music and being a musician during my last two years at The Lyric Opera in Chicago. He had been an assistant conductor to Arturo Toscanini at La Scala and his students included Claudio Abbado as well as Ricardo Muti.

Antonino Votto was many times a collaborator with Callas in productions at La Scala and on legendary studio recordings with her. He was an inspiration for everyone who came in contact with him.

What I remember most about him was his careful attention to musical and dramatic detail combined with what seemed like an effortless and completely unpretentious approach to making music; it made everything appear to be easy and natural.

Maestro Votto once said to the orchestra during a rehearsal, "This is a strange business. I stand here wave my arms having a good time listening to you and I get the credit!"

If I may I will offer a personal conjecture about the important difference between Tullio Serafin and Antonino Votto. For me, Serafin was a teacher of performers and Votto taught conductors and was a collaborator with performers. One was not better than the other. I would love some day to meet Muti and ask him what it was like to study with Antonino Votto.

Tell me a little bit about Dmitri Mitropoulos.

Oh, yes, this is fun! I joke about Mitropoulos being my first major conductor; that with Mitropoulos I started at the top and worked my way down. It is just silly when I say that. I must have been nineteen years old at the time—or younger—and an extra in the orchestra, not a permanent player.

With Mitropoulos, I believe the opera was *Girl of the Golden West*.[11] He was amazing, because he had a legendary photographic memory. While he was conducting, he seemed to be looking at a vision of the score in the air. On occasion, he paused, perhaps to flip through the pages of his imaginary score. I remember one time in particular he stopped and said, "Oh, second horn, that's an F#." He knew every note from looking at the score in his mind. Incredible.

But it's not only the memory. He had a musicality, a profound musicianship that was always evident. It was just relentless. Every phrase that he conducted, every little moment in the score, was important. It certainly was to him— that was obvious. He knew the score; he knew the material. I cannot claim to know music intricately, as he did. He was a superbly gifted and committed artist. After my experience of working with him, I would never even dream of becoming a conductor. Forget about it.

What about Sir Georg Solti?

You mention Solti, and I must laugh. Solti irritated me, because he wanted me always to play bigger, more emotionally and more extroverted. I understand now a little better than I did then, but he had the blowtorch on all the time. Such intensity. The flame was all-consuming. I understand now the necessity for intensity. But then, having to confront it all the time was just too much for me.

On one occasion I had a brief solo, five notes. I will never forget, he leaned over to me during rehearsal and yelled, "Play it like a concerto!" I mean, five notes? Come on. But I now appreciate what he meant. I must have sounded naïve and uninvolved. I was certainly shy. You know, very often shyness has the appearance of indifference. It may have seemed to Solti that I didn't care. But, of course, just the opposite was the case. I see students who care desperately, but they are afraid—afraid to open up. And so they appear to act casual and uninvolved, when nothing could be further from the truth. They are afraid of failing.

Occasionally, in young performers I see an attempt to convey a casual demeanor; so they stand oddly, with heels on the stage and toes up. It looks like they don't care. But they care so much—maybe too much—that they are actually afraid. I advise performers to work on stance and never to adopt a posture that looks like you are in a bar just hanging out. Stage presence and the visual element are essential. Show the listener, from your appearance on stage, that you do care. That you believe what you are doing is important.

What can you recall about Leopold Stokowski?

For three years, I played English horn with Stokowski in the American Symphony Orchestra,[12] which he founded. When Stokowski conducted,

---

11 *La Fanciulla del West* ("The Girl of the Golden West") is an opera written in 1910 by Giacomo Puccini.

12 A New York-based orchestra, founded in 1962.

he projected a sense of entitlement. It was very impressive to be in his presence. He was not quite as overt as Solti, but he did want me to play loudly all the time. Projecting the sound of the English horn loudly into a hall is difficult, because it is in the middle timbre of the orchestra. It can be easily buried, even within the oboe section. So, too often the English horn can scarcely be heard.

My teacher, Robert Bloom,[13] had played English horn with Stokowski in the Philadelphia Orchestra, I believe in the 1930s. Because I was studying with Bloom at the same time that I was playing with Stokowski, I complained during my lessons about what "Stoki" wanted. Bloom said to me, "Oh, it is always the same. He wanted me to play too loud." This reminds me of the time I was driving from having dinner with Bob and his wife Sarah on I-91 between New Haven and Hartford, and I saw a car the had a bumper sticker that read, "Honk if you play oboe". Somehow I got a copy of that sticker and mailed it to Bloom as a joke. A few days later, he sent me back the bumper sticker having written on it with a red Magic Marker, "DON'T!" And he meant it.

Stokowski had less overt technical skill than Mitropoulos or Solti, but he had an absolutely incredible sense of the magic of the moment and an ability to create that magic by balancing all the elements of the color of the sound. This is what pianists call *voicing*. I realize I'm contradicting myself, but he wanted the English horn in its solos really to rise above the sound of the rest of the orchestra. If you want to hear that magic, listen to his studio recording of the *Swan of Tuonela* with my teacher Robert Bloom playing English horn. It is a legendary recording and quintessential Stokowski, a perfect example of pure mystical magic.

Nevertheless, playing too loudly all the time was uninteresting for me. One Sunday afternoon at an important concert at Carnegie Hall, I decided, "Oh, forget about it. I am just going to do what *I* want." So I started playing prettily, rather than loudly. It drove him crazy! This was during the concert. He came close to screaming at me, with his arms flailing wildly about, urging me to get louder; more, more, more. I didn't respond to his demands. I just played it as nicely as I wished.

Afterward, I felt really guilty. I had been playing with his orchestra for three years. But I was doing enough freelance work to manage financially without this orchestra job. So, I went backstage and confessed to him, "Maestro, I need to talk to you. I feel terrible. My performance today was ridiculous, unforgivable. I think I should leave the orchestra because I am uncomfortable playing the way you want me to play." He was wonderful. He said, "Oh, young man, don't worry, I will teach you. I will show you how to do it." He was a nurturing, kind and supportive teacher.

But at that point I just had enough. So I said, "You know, Maestro, it is not that I can't do it or that I don't know what you want. I know what you want, and I can do it. But I don't like to play that way." Then I thought, "Oh no, I'm in deep trouble." So I said, "Okay, Maestro, if the composer

13 Robert Bloom (1908–1994), renowned oboist, composer and teacher, born in Pennsylvania.

wanted what you are asking me to do, he would have given this part to the trombone, not the English horn."

Bravo!

His eyebrows went up to the ceiling, and he said, "Young man, I think you are right. We should part ways." He found another English horn player.

What was the story with the Houston Symphony Orchestra?

Maestro Stokowski had actually asked me to move to Houston to be his principal oboist. I didn't want to leave New York for a variety of personal reasons including that I just—well, like a lot of people—I had the New York virus. I had to be in New York where so much was happening, and I needed to be a part of that.

New York is perhaps the greatest collection of creative minds in the world. I love wonderful cities, like Paris. And London I absolutely adore, and many other places, like Beijing or Chicago! But when you see the sheer number of creative people in New York, and our system of government allowing a freedom of creativity that is astonishing, I couldn't leave the city. I couldn't go to Houston. In those days, Houston was a small town. I used to joke at the time that everything in Houston was not indigenous or internal, but imported from Detroit.

I must tell you the epilogue to the English horn story, what came after with Leopold Stokowski.

About a year after I quit his orchestra, I got a call from an influential contractor, Loren Glickman, an important person in the New York musical scene. He did most of the contracting for what we call pick-up orchestras and important recording dates. Loren called me and said, "We're doing a recording. I need you to come and play English horn. And we are doing Bach transcriptions." I said, "Bach transcriptions? Stokowski must be conducting." He said, "Yes."

So, I said, "Oh, Loren, wait a minute. I don't think you want me on that recording session." I told him the whole story of my quitting Stokowski's orchestra and was afraid Stokowski would still be angry. Loren then said to me, "Don't worry about it. He won't remember you." I said, "What do you mean? I played in that orchestra with him for three years." Loren said, "He doesn't remember anyone who is not important to him. And you are obviously not important to him anymore." So, I said, "Well, okay, I'll do it. But you have to allow me a substitute waiting near a telephone, in case he throws me out." I paid for the sub out of my own pocket in advance.

So I went to the record date. Stokowski looked right through me, like I was a piece of plexiglass. He had no recollection of me at all. And so we recorded. Of course, he had electronic means to control the volume and balance in the studio. During the session, he was very complimentary and afterward he actually included my name on the record jacket. About ten years ago I stumbled upon the LP in a Salvation Army Thrift Shop on sale for twenty-five cents, thinking to myself, "I'm already a has-been." So, in the end, it all turned out well. I idolized him, of course.

May I ask you about Stokowski's conducting style? He famously conducted without a baton, as did some other conductors, Karajan and Celibidache, for example. How did this affect the orchestra's cohesion? Was Stokowski difficult to follow? What are the advantages and disadvantages of playing under a conductor without a baton?

Rhythmic clarity was not particularly Stokowski's strength. His strength was color and dynamics and a kind of fluid rubato. He blurred the rhythmic pulse, which helped him provide a cushion of sound. Not everything was totally precise. Karajan may have conducted similarly and Celibidache, too. I think Karajan and Celibidache knew what they were doing, and did so deliberately, whereas with Stokowski, it was just in his ear. In fact, I believe Karajan would from time to time use a baton. The result is a more blended experience without the baton. Without the benefit of a baton, the orchestra seems to have less crystalline accuracy, but this was Stokowski's artistic voice. It helped him make the magic. Not using a baton made the sonority a little more blurred and vulnerable. Let's not forget that he was also an organist. It gave Stokowski the color he wanted. It was great. Incredible privilege to be a part of it!

Stokowski had another gift that was rare. Within about six minutes in front of any orchestra, it sounded like his orchestra. It didn't matter, it could be the Chicago Symphony, New York Philharmonic or whomever, even what we call a pick-up orchestra put together just for that one occasion. The orchestra took on the color and homogenous texture that he was famous for. It had what became known as "The Philadelphia sound," the Stokowski sound. He said nothing and did nothing overt. It has to have had something to do with the subtle way he moved his body. No one could figure out what he did. One of his most often directions to individual players simply was, "Do better, do better!"

The only other conductor I can remember who had this magical ability of completely changing the sound of a group was Robert Shaw. Within a few minutes every group of singers sounded like The Robert Shaw Choral. It was mystical to be in the presence of that experience as well. I got to see and hear it with both conductors.

All great conductors know what they want. Good or bad, you can agree with them or not, it does not matter: they are conducting. They come to the rehearsal and performance with an educated, informed commitment of what they believe the composer wants.

Peter Magg, the great Mozart conductor, had very simple instructions for the orchestra that profoundly changed the sound and inflection. I never forget and use his instructions with my students. He said, "In Mozart there are two kinds of accents: inter-muscular and intravenous." Of course, what he was trying to get is the difference between an accent that was plush and cushiony from and accent that had a pinch. It is hard to explain how much that simple instruction changed the inflection of the phrase.

I remember, years ago I was interviewed by June LeBell and Robert Sherman on WQXR in New York. In a particular interview with Robert Sherman I was late for the 10 a.m. air time. I can't believe I did that. He was very nice to me, anyway, but because I was late I came in the middle of an important subject, which was, "How does a great conductor communicate with the orchestra?" I was so flustered that I just said, "It's the eyes." You know when you look into a conductor's eyes if they know what you are trying to do and you know if you're doing what they want." I don't need the beat. I don't need the baton. I need the eyes. I need to look into the conductor's eyes and know that he knows what I'm trying to do, and that we have total communication. If he wants me to change the phrase, I can see in the eyes where he would like me to go. It was a totally off-the-cuff answer, but there still is not a better answer that I know.

Stokowski was famous for being known among his orchestra players as having "Fish eyes." Fritz Reiner was the same. It was frightening. Alfredo Antonini, who conducted the CBS Philharmonic, once said to me when I made a wrong entrance, "Lucca, don't worry. When you have to come in, I look at you, I smile and you play." The orchestra of some of New York's most illustrious musicians fell on the floor laughing.

There it is again and again; it's the eyes. Has nothing to do with the "stick" or baton technique. I have seen great conductors lead performances with a baton that seemingly had nothing to do with what was going on. I remember one well-known conductor conducting the Bernstein *Jeremiah Symphony*, which has a movement in seven-quarter time, which is a bit unusual. It typically could be conducted in 2-2-3 or 2-3-2 or 3-2-2, per measure. He said, "I have the solution for this awkward meter. We will count it 1,2,3,4,5,6, **SEV-UN.**" Which of course simplified it to be eight beats to the measure. I'll never tell who that was.

On the other hand, there are great conductors who are acutely aware of every flick of the stick. But all the good ones have those eyes. I tell my students, "Memorize your solos and look directly at the conductor's eyes." In any case it makes them at least think you care about what they want. Conducting an orchestra has to be one of the most insecure feelings in the world. People judge you on sounds that you do not make. It is bizarre!

Remember that Antonino Votto once said to the orchestra during a rehearsal, "This is a strange business. I stand here wave my arms having a good time listening to you and I get the credit!" In some cases, the blame.

Chapter 3. Performance

Seoul: During performance in 1999, Photo by Yea Jin Studio

Daniel Pereira: *May I ask you about concentration during performance, points of focus, the way we listen, the way we should listen, and the psychological implications of sustaining concentration?*

Humbert Lucarelli: Yes. Okay, maintaining concentration. One of the problems is the ease with which the mind wanders. For me, concentration is like meditation. You learn not to get upset when the mind wanders but calmly return to focus.

Onstage and in general we exist on several levels. When I perform sometimes, I find myself engaged in inner criticism, wondering, "What does the audience think of me?" "Am I walking correctly?" "How do I look?" "Am I thinking correctly?" "Am I moving correctly?" "Do they like my clothes?" "Am I sharp?" "That interval wasn't clean." Such pitfalls may be common to all of us. And then, on another level we think about the music. Of course, the goal is to move so far into the music that nothing else exists. I love the sensation of no longer existing outside the music. In fact, I sometimes listen detached to the sound coming out from the instrument, not so much consciously involved in the act of creating the sound, but more in observing it. That is a most wonderful moment, don't you think? As Mike Nichols[14] has said, "The best thing about having total control is having none."

I learned so much about creating the best conditions for concentration when I went on the Bach Aria Group tour as a substitute for my teacher and mentor Robert Bloom. Observing the difference of how the two female singers prepared for the performances was an inspiring lesson. Soprano, Lois Marshal spent the whole day in her hotel room on the day of a performance. She didn't even answer the phone. Maureen Forrester was all over the place, in the lobby, in the restaurant of the hotel having lunch with

---

14 Mike Nichols (b. 1931), German-born American filmmaker.

friends, shopping. She found her center by defusing before a performance. They were so different. I had to figure out what worked best for me. There clearly is no "one way" to do it.

I agree. So, you think that we should, as you say, detach from the action; almost as an out-of-body experience?

Completely. Yes. I think I told you one time that I used to practice in front of a full-length mirror, visualizing my image in the mirror doing the performing. One time I remember wanting to set up a mirror for your hands while you were playing piano, so that you could pretend that the sound came from the mirror not from your hands. This is a wonderful technique to practice and to enjoy a kind of remote control.

As a pianist, I recently discovered that my eyes—my sight—can get too much in the way. I sometimes practice blindfolded or with my eyes closed.

Oh, yes.

And I realized that my aural skills improved. Is this the case with oboe playing as well?

Yes, completely. Even with eyes open, I don't see. I look at nothing. It's an absolutely wonderful technique. I mean, certainly people who are blind can play beautifully. Visual stimuli can be a distraction. And it is fun. Sometimes, during Alexander Technique, I was instructed to keep my eyes open. Not that I'm looking at anything in particular, but the eyes provide an anchor, in a way. Ballet dancers maintain their balance, by looking at the exit sign in the back of the hall. They don't so much look at the words; it is just a focal point. It helps. It gives you an anchor.

How do you concentrate before a concert? What do you do or what happens during your day, the three or four hours before the performance?

For me the routine is really important. I eat breast of chicken, just a simple broiled breast of chicken, and a little bit of bread, not too much food, but enough so that I'm not hungry when I play, because hunger weakens me and makes me dizzy. So, I must have some protein. Some performers eat bananas to help with the nerves. Some eat salads. But I find that hard to digest; my stomach doesn't want it.

On the day of a concert I like to iron my own pants. It's like I tell my students, a ritual of practicing, of doing your own laundry. You clean the music. You clean your own clothes. You do it in private, not in public.

Some people talk about taking a shower before every concert, to remove the garbage of the music business so as to wash it away. That's a wonderful idea. I do that, to go to the concert stage physically and spiritually cleansed.

This reminds me of comments by Andre Agassi,[15] in his autobiography Open. He said that, before his games, he showered six times at least. It seems almost like an

---

15   Andre Agassi (b. 1970), a retired American tennis player.

electrical thing. The water discharges you of electrical impulses, and so one relaxes.

For sure. Before a concert, I must shower with very hot water, almost so the skin starts to feel like it's burning. It is a cleansing. It washes worldly things away.

Yes, it does. And so, on the day of a concert, do you listen to music? How do you find the inspiration, or do you just not think about it?

No, I personally can't think about it on the day of the performance, because I want the moment of impact on stage to be the first explosion. I've done my homework days before, weeks and even maybe years before. On the day of the concert, whatever is going to come out will come out. That's it. Basta.[16] On the day of the concert, I need to save it. It's like cooking a dinner or preparing for any important experience. You can't think about it too much before. and then it can become calculated. But you must be prepared and plan to be open, in fact embrace the unexpected. You just are prepared to go; you hold back, you hold back. It's like cooking a delicious dinner. Timing is everything. In front of the audience, you are overtaken by the music and the moment. And then, at the perfect moment, it comes together. I believe it's one of the reasons so many good musicians love to cook. A great chef, Daniel Orr told me once, "Some of the best recipes are from mistakes."

Yes, ideally.

In fact, I've often thought of programming for a recital as if it is like preparing a great dinner. It has to have an appetizer, a pasta dish, a serious entrée, a salad and a desert. The encore is maybe the after-dinner drink. Maybe not always in that order, but it may have a variety, or an interesting sequence. It could even be one-dimensional. It just has to have some thought behind the whole experience. Remember a recital is after all a recitation of the persona of the performer. It is not simply an arbitrary set of pieces. I think maybe I'm going too far with this analogy. Stop me.

I am also a bit superstitious. I have to confess that one of my superstitions is I like wearing red underwear when I perform, because I believe that red keeps jealousy away. I even do this at dress rehearsals, because in a dress rehearsal, everything should be the same as in the performance—including the clothes I wear—so I feel comfortable when I perform. A famous singer I knew wore new undergarments every time she was performing a new piece she had not performed before.

But, you know, I think the question you ask goes a little deeper than it seems. Although the externals seem trivial they are not. They create an environment in which you can do what you need and hope to do. You must create the environment for the cathartic moment to happen. I suppose that's why some musicians even insist that the dress rehearsal occurs on the actual stage where they are going to perform.

Let me explain to you the sensation of creating a "bubble" around yourself. I have defined a space around my whole body. That's my private place—

---

16   Italian word for "it's enough."

where I live. My acting teacher once said to me, "Try to create a bubble that always surrounds you as you perform." It's like the "transporter" in *Star Trek*. You must recreate that sensation every time and be transported.

Recently, I sent you a YouTube video of Sergiu Celibidache, the Romanian conductor, performing Ravel's Bolero. It is an incredible performance, filled with vitality and risk-taking. Has taking risks been lost over the years? Now it seems that performers more minutely control every aspect of the execution, with no room remaining for improvisation.

The fear of being wrong is the performer's biggest enemy. So many performers want to sound like a mannequin with a kind of cosmetic perfection. We musicians must stand in front of an audience and risk looking foolish and even sometimes grotesque. But the audience loves it. It makes us human. It seems to me that Celibidache had a face and soul like a mountain, with the lines like valleys and the whole character of nature. You can't help but loving him. Instantaneous communication. Leonard Bernstein made intense use of his eyes. He conducted with his eyes, his eyebrows, and his entire face. Celibidache did, too; he believed in himself.

Yes. In your extensive performing career, have you ever slipped outside yourself while playing, feeling like another person, or governed by some external energy?

Yes, it's a great sensation. When I get there, I know I'm playing well.

Other than your own?

Yes. You make several suggestions. The notion of being dominated by an external energy is profound. And feeling outside yourself is powerful. I like to feel as if I breathe the air in the concert hall and in the audience, and try to sense the positive energy in the room. I love the idea of being disembodied—controlling and observing at the same time. It's not direct control but more like a remote control from a distance. I see and hear myself coming off the walls of the hall. In a good performance I don't know if I'm the performer or the audience.

After all is said and done, most people attend a concert because they want to have a good time; to enjoy themselves. They want to hear something that moves them. Go with them.

Too often, we try to perfect our performance. Perfection becomes the focus of our effort. We fear being wrong. You can never do anything important if you are afraid of being wrong. Certainly you must be aware. I don't want to play wrong notes, but being preoccupied with technical perfection cannot be the ultimate focus of the performance.

If I'm performing in fear, I can't let go. I have to hold on to the performance instead of letting go. In a book I recently read, *The Talent Code*, the author Daniel Coyle gave an explanation of performing. Why do I practice? So I don't have to think when I am in front of the audience, so I can just let go—although he explains the contradiction of the importance of thinking during performances. Part of me is listening, analyzing—and being disappointed with any part of the execution that hasn't measured up to what I wanted to do. But I cannot let that self-observation destroy the moment. Maybe once in a while I can say to myself, "Oh, that's not so bad." Almost never happens.

Performers will grow only if they listen to themselves while playing. They must do this. But where is the line between listening, being self-analytical and, at the same time, letting go? Quite a challenge! You know what I'm talking about?

Clearly.

Reaching that level of multi-dimensional awareness is very difficult. We cannot be one-dimensional. We must exist on several levels.

This also speaks to one of your previous questions, about concentration during performance. While performing, my mind zigzags. I think all over the place—about the F#, about the color of the note, about this or that interval, and about whether I am really speaking—wondering if the audience gets what I am saying. So my mind is going "bang-bang-bang-bang-bang-bang," like billiard balls on a pool table.

Performing is just like watching a game of pool. I see all those balls moving. But I am not looking at just one ball. I am, in fact, seeing the whole complexity, allowing my body to absorb all of the stimuli coming at me, all at one time.

As far as you can remember, what were your most incredible screw-ups during a live performance?

Oh. There are so many choices. A favorite of mine: Once, in an orchestra playing Delius' The Walk to Paradise Garden, I became completely engrossed in the sound and its beauty. As I continued to listen, becoming more and more immersed, it occurred to me that something was missing. And then I suddenly realized, "It's me! I should have been playing!"

Blatant wrong notes are so stupid. I know better. When that happens, I wonder, "Where did that come from? Who did that?" I lose concentration. Concentration need not be intellectual. It comes from hours of practice and deeply knowing the piece. It's like singing *Happy Birthday.* You don't make a mistake. Playing the Strauss Oboe Concerto has to become the same as singing *Happy Birthday.* It should not even occur to you to play a wrong note. It takes a long time to get to that place.

Oh, I remember one incident that was actually fun. I was afraid of a fast movement in a Telemann partita. It was technically so challenging that I opted to perform it a little too slowly in the performance. As I played, I knew that my tempo was completely wrong. So, at the end, I stopped and just said to the audience, "You know, I can take that faster, the way it should be played." So I did. It was at Lincoln Center, in fact, at Alice Tully Hall. The audience went berserk. They completely loved and enjoyed my honesty.

Other mistakes I have made? Once, I walked on stage with my fly open. I'll never forget that! But I think you must be willing to appear foolish onstage. The audience will forgive you any peculiarity if you are honest. I simply shrugged and zipped up my fly. The audience applauded. Getting your mind and your spirit into a place of no judgment and allowing the performance to happen authentically are necessary—and difficult.

I have seen and heard some wonderful players who are at one with the music, who allow the composer just to take them. I sometimes call it "submitting to the composer." That may be the wrong expression. But allowing the moment to happen. Over a prolonged period, it's hard to do. You can do it sometimes for about twenty seconds, thirty seconds, or even just five. You can do it for a minute. After that, the mind wants to get in the way.

What about the psychological elements of performance? Addressing these is essential. Claudio Arrau, the Chilean pianist, said that psychoanalysis was fundamental to his life and his art. So he underwent psychoanalytic therapy, to improve his mindfulness. He believed self-awareness to be decisive in the life of a performer. Do you agree? Or can performing excellence—sitting at the piano, playing an instrument, or singing—occur without the artist undergoing some psychoanalytic discovery?

Yes, psychological elements in performance are essential, but no, performers need not undergo psychoanalysis. It's very individual. If we are going to speak, we must know who we are, and if we have anything to say.

Let me go a couple places here. First, problems with saying something or not may arise, because we are afraid that we have nothing to say. We must first get over this. Second, in order to determine where we are going, we must know our origins. I suppose that is why psychoanalysis can be helpful for some people. History is so important. It reminds me of a rocket. A rocket has energy to propel it, but, unless we understand its origin, we can't send it in the right direction. So, we are unable to express ourselves unless we know who our "selves" are.

Sadly, most of us, myself included, are essentially dissatisfied with ourselves. We would like to be better people. We would like to be more intelligent. We would like to feel more deeply. I am most unhappy with myself when I have not understood when I'm insensitive to the person I am with—no, not that word understood—when I have not *appreciated* the person who is with me. I would like to have more craft in everything I do.

And so, in discussion with someone, I try to make a point. My inability to explain my point adequately is my fault; my responsibility. Especially with students this is true. Forgive me, but I must say this. Some teachers believe that when a student doesn't understand what the teacher is saying, the student is untalented. *I don't think so.*

If a student fails to understand my point, I have failed to connect. In order to connect, I must know where that student is, and I must be focused, centered, as a person. In order to accomplish this, I must trust myself.

Well; now you are moving to another subject that I planned to bring up: your teaching experience.

So, we go back to performance? But we must not forget that performing is teaching, and teaching is performance. What does it mean, anyway, to know myself?

Know who you are, know what you want and know where you wish to go.

And all of those concepts that you are talking about are often non-verbal. We don't always know who we are, what we want or where we wish to go.

I have always believed that the performer—actually, any human being— must be open to change, must be flexible. He or she must be willing to adapt. Knowing ourselves doesn't necessarily mean that we are complete. We can't sit back and relax.

Exactly. And the same is expected of the audience. Listeners must be open and willing to change.

We change continually.

Correct, every moment. So, in teaching, I avoid keeping a log of a student's lessons—writing what transpired in the previous lesson—because the following week a different person walks into the room.

I have to be sensitive and open to that. Change is critical. We must believe in change. My nephew hates change. He's terrified of it. I keep saying to him, "Joe, the only constant in the world is change. You have to embrace it and love it, be amused by it, be moved by it. You have to laugh at yourself, including your resistance to change."

You have performed in so many countries, including China. Can you recall some of your experiences in the Far East?

I love being in Asia. I could live in Beijing. It's a deceptively easy city. I traveled there with one of my students who made my stay very comfortable. I visited his grandfather and grandmother, who lived in a simple, humble apartment. They were incredibly beautiful people. It was outrageous to me that we were able to communicate on a very meaningful level. Many years later my student's aunt told him that I had changed her life. Amazing.

While there, I was invited to give master classes during a two-week period at the Central Conservatory, which is considered the "Juilliard" of China. We also went to Tianjin, an extraordinary place. It is a city of many artisans— painters and sculptors—and antique dealers. Its citizens place high value on aesthetic endeavor. China is a fascinating country. I could feel its ancient roots everywhere.

I also loved South Korea. Mr. Young-Ju Park, who founded Egon, an international company making wood products, presented me in a concert series there in different cities. We did approximately fifteen concerts in one month and made a CD of two live performances that were done in Seoul. He has produced these concerts over many years throughout

South Korea, as a gesture of support for his workers. What an unusually wonderful person.

In Australia, I did the East Coast tour—Sydney and Melbourne, even going to Tasmania, which was incredible. There is so little pollution there that the colors of the landscape, when you are outside, almost hurt your eyes. The orchestras throughout Australia were very good.

To reach Australia, I was routed via Greece, where there was a three-day layover in Athens. When I was ready to leave for Australia, I was told that I was not in compliance with cholera immunization, so I was barred from the plane. As a result, there were eight additional days in Athens, four days waiting for the shot, and then another four waiting for it to take effect. That's when the photograph of me at the Parthenon was taken, which has been used as a cover for recordings and magazines.

The whole incident was disastrous because I arrived four days late in Sydney, where my tour started by my performing the Strauss Concerto with the Sydney Philharmonic at the Opera House. I touched down at 7 a.m. for a 10 a.m. rehearsal of the concerto, after a fourteen-hour flight. It was just bananas. In rehearsal, I couldn't even stand. They brought me a little stool to sit on, after not playing for four days. I couldn't have been in worse condition to play the Strauss, which is a very demanding test of endurance. My body felt that I had a million ants going around in it. But I got through it. Afterward, I was still breathing, and so the sun came up the next day. I did not get a very good review for my first concert, but later things got better.

The Hungarian pianist Lili Kraus,[17] who lived in America for many years, was an incredible artist. You played in a freelance orchestra, the name of which I can't remember, for a concert series that she headlined, as soloist for all of the Mozart concerti. Do you recall that occasion?

Kraus was a mystic. When she took a breath, she took inside her body all the wonderful energy in the room. She could make magic happen in a moment. She could turn it on like a light switch. Seeing her and watching her absorb energy taught me a lot, the importance of trying to find that magic.

We did the concerts at Town Hall, when it was still being used for classical music. We performed two or three concerti each night for the entire season. How many concerti did Mozart compose, twenty-six?

He wrote twenty-seven concerti, but one is for three pianos, and one is for two.

So you see, I'm not a scholar. I can't remember how many piano concerti Mozart wrote. She had done a recording of all of them. The concerts were presented to promote the recording. One rehearsal was particularly memorable. A workman had come into the hall where we were rehearsing and began to vacuum in the balcony. She looked up at the balcony, and I thought she was going to ask him to stop. Instead, a little smile came over her face, and she suddenly became engrossed in her playing with the most

---

17   Lili Kraus (1903–1986), Hungarian pianist.

powerful, intense concentration you could imagine. She just turned her playing on, as I say, like a light switch. And she got his attention. The worker turned off the vacuum cleaner, sat down, and listened to her play for the rest of the rehearsal.

During one week I played first with her at Town Hall and then in Boston. Then, in Philadelphia that same week with a third orchestra, she was again the soloist. Noticing me sitting in all of the orchestras, she asked, "Are you following me around?" I said to her, "What are you doing? You're playing everywhere. You can't do that. It's not good for you. Why are you playing everywhere?" She gave me a candid reply and said, "Because I'm afraid, if I don't, someone else will." She accepted every engagement.

You have played first or second oboe in orchestras in such important venues as the Metropolitan Opera House and Avery Fisher Hall, both in New York City. What is it like, playing orchestral music in a major concert hall in terms of acoustics?

For me the most beautiful acoustics were at Carnegie Hall in the early years of my career, while playing English horn under Stokowski. The Carnegie Hall acoustics were magnificent. The sound had texture and depth and you knew it was reaching the listeners. Resorting to dynamic extremes to get the sound into the hall was unnecessary. We could play almost as if we were sitting in our own living rooms. The sound invariably projected all the way to the back of the hall.

The Carnegie Hall stage was too high; too much distance between the stage and the audience. Listeners in the first few rows had to stretch uncomfortably in order to see. So they redesigned the hall's interior, and one of the things they did was lowered the stage. The acoustic result was not so good, I think, because the stage was pulled away from the ceiling. It changed the reverberation. It also changed the amount of space underneath the stage, so especially double bass and cello players who put their instruments' pegs on the stage floor could not get the same depth of vibration from the reduced space underneath the stage. It caused many problems. But it still remains one of the great halls of the world. I also played solo recitals in Carnegie. Bizarrely, I made my Carnegie debut in what we used to call "the big hall" now The Isaac Stern Hall with my own rock band. It was called *Musamorphosis*. We started with Renaissance music and ended with heavy metal. The whole group was made up of brilliant and incredibly talented Juilliard graduates who taught me a lot about myself. This has to classify as one of the many sins of my youth.

At Avery Fisher Hall, I played principal and second oboe many times and even concerti with orchestra. Playing principal, in its first week of inaugural concerts, I could barely hear the second oboe player, who sat right next to me. On the other hand, I could hear one viola player who was maybe ten feet away. That viola sounded just like a buzz saw in my ear.

As originally constructed—it was such an avoidance of the issue—the walls were built with screens in front and movable panels behind, so they could "tune" the hall and fix their mistakes by adjusting the panels. Forgive me, I don't want to use the word, but in my opinion, it was artificial. The whole idea was useless.

Then, they did the first renovation of the hall. When Stokowski was asked what he thought of the change, he was reported to have said, "Well, you know, that hall has always been a problem. It's like a woman with artificial legs, artificial hair, an artificial arm, one eye, and a pimple on her nose. They removed the pimple." That was his devastating comment about the hall.

Everyone was critical about the Avery Fisher acoustics and with good reason. I think it has been redone now three or four times. Now the Hall has an almost electronic sound, not quite acoustic. Someone said that Avery Fisher made his fame building high-fidelity and stereophonic audio systems, and that the Hall now sounds "like an inexpensive Avery Fisher hi-fi unit."

It has been reported recently that they are going to redo it again. The fear is that they are throwing good money after bad. For me, the shape of the hall is simply not good. It's too long and narrow, and too high at the rear. I don't know if they can get somebody to fix it. I certainly hope so.

The Metropolitan Opera House acoustics, even from the pit, are much better than those at Avery Fisher. I played at the Met many times with The Royal Ballet. The people who built the Metropolitan Opera House did a good job. The acoustics there are very good. In spite of the fact that the hall is quite large, you can still hear everything. The acoustics in the New York State Theater on the other hand—now the Koch Theater—are not as good. The State Theater was designed for dancers; the sound is meant in part to hide the sound of their feet as they are dancing on stage. So, it's a little dead and not hospitable for live instrumental performances. I am always impressed when I hear friends of mine play there and sound good.

You never know how these halls are finally designed, developed and built. The builders seem never to get advice from the right people. Ask a second violin player in any orchestra, he would build a really great hall; but no. These acousticians come to it knowing so much and…forgive my sarcasm and frustration. I have played in some wonderful venues that are new, so I know it is possible to build a new hall with good acoustics.

I don't mean to talk so fast in a circle but it's an important subject. We musicians spend our lives trying to develop a sound. You know that. You have developed a special sound, one of the best pianistic sounds I know. And I have worked on improving my sound for my entire life. And then I play in a hall that obstructs all of my effort. It is discouraging. You can't win. Forgive me. In the end, the real disaster is that bad acoustics turn off an audience. They think they are hearing the music, and they are not. A recording sounds better than the live experience. I have heard many people say they see no reason to come back. They hear it better on a recording.

There is another aspect that is overlooked and that is from the performer's perspective. When you hear yourself in a good hall, you are inspired. I remember my teacher Bloom once when we were playing in a dead hall saying during a rehearsal how badly he felt playing there, and someone who was listening in the hall said it sounded good out there. Bloom replied, "But I'm up here!"

You notice in rock concerts the performers have what we call monitors on stage, speakers that let them hear the fully mixed sound that the audience is hearing. It makes them play better.

Chapter 4. The Audience

Lark Quintet, ca: 1965
on the roof of the Apthorp Apartments, at 79th and Broadway, NYC
John Wion, Flute; Arthur Bloom, Clarinet; Jerry Warsaw, French Horn;
Alan Brown, Bassoon; Humbert Lucarelli, Oboe

Daniel Pereira: *Bert, do audiences behave differently from one country to another?*

Humbert Lucarelli: Certainly, I would say that audience behavior does vary from country to country. Sometimes variations exist even within a country. I experienced this during a concert that I will never forget when my quintet played at a military academy. The cadets were trained not to applaud after each piece. It was their protocol. So, at the end of a piece, if they liked it, they all clapped simultaneously once. One clap, just one clap. It was peculiar.

In my experience in Japan, audiences applauded only briefly after each piece, but enthusiastically at the end of the concert. Even if they liked an individual piece or soloist very much, they applauded only to escort us off the stage. But at the end of the concert—if they enjoyed the concert, of course—we could expect a standing ovation. Because I was a soloist in the middle of the program, they brought me back to the stage to take a final bow after the end of the concert, so that the audience could show its appreciation. In retrospect, I would say that the Japanese might be reticent about making public displays of any sort or showing appreciation for one performer more than another. This speaks to another funny theory of mine that people who live on an island do not want to impose on one another.

To answer your question, I could go with the cliché and say that, in general, Italian audiences are warmer and more extroverted, whereas German audiences are more formal. I don't know. That's a tough question.

So, are you thinking stereotypically?

Yes, generally Italians are thought to be warm people, although they can also be critical. If they are dissatisfied, they boo, which happens rarely in America. During a concert, Italians may even shout out to express pleasure or disdain. As a young boy, my father was taken to hear Aïda at La Scala in Milan. He told me, at the point when the tenor sang "Aïda, where are you?"

someone in the audience yelled out "She went to poop." Someone else screamed, "She went to find a conductor."

Only once did I witness such a spectacle in New York—someone in the audience yelling to express displeasure at a tenor who was at the Metropolitan Opera. It was embarrassing; insulting. The singer was one of the famous, great "Three Tenors," not Pavarotti. He sang beautifully.

Carreras, perhaps?

Yes, it was Carreras, exactly right. A heckler in the audience yelled, "Bravo, Bergonzi!"[18] So Carreras gave him the finger, what the New York Times has called "the international symbol of disrespect." The audience loved it. It was a magical moment of a powerful dialogue between the audience and the performer. It was an unfair heckling. Carreras was right. Carreras is not Bergonzi, and Bergonzi is not Carreras. José Carreras is a great artist and does not deserve that kind of broad criticism.

More heckling occurs in Italy. New York audiences tend to be polite. Even if they are dissatisfied, they will offer at least polite applause. European audiences, in general, tend to be more honest about displaying their feelings when they applaud. English audiences are reserved if they don't like a performance. They applaud, but very little. The French are likewise reserved. In Asia—in Korea—they were very warm to me, much like the Italians.

I have lived in America for about thirteen years and performed here frequently as well as attended many concerts in such cities as New York, Boston and Washington, D.C. I have developed the impression that audiences in America are easy to please, and standing ovations are almost a must. They usually happen immediately after the last note of the performance and do not last long. Have you found that to be the case?

Yes, I think so. American audiences are not so much easy to please, as they are very supportive. How much they wish to show their pleasure often surprises me. It is a good sign that Americans tend to be so appreciative. I think it is genuine. It doesn't mean they are not discerning. In fact, the level of appreciation sometimes shocks me. I think, "Oh man, that was not a good concert," but the audience was still kind. The audience wants to have a good time. They have left the comfort of their home and paid money to have a good time. It is a totally positive experience.

I am also surprised when people say, "Americans don't like classical music. They don't go to classical music concerts." I don't see that. I see quite the opposite. In Chicago, when I was a kid ushering at Orchestra Hall, the audience received the Chicago Symphony almost like today's sports figures. Enthusiasm was everywhere. It was beautiful. Seeing that audiences could feel so strongly for a performer made me want to become a musician. It meant that being a performing musician was important.

---

18 Carlo Bergonzi (b.1924), Italian opera singer.

I completely agree with the idea that American audiences are supportive of the artists and grateful to the orchestras and soloists. But a standing ovation should be given only for something truly special, for a performance of a much higher standard, don't you think?

Yes. Seeing a true ovation, with everyone enthusiastic and standing, is profound; you can feel it. I love it. I played with Samuel Baron in the Bach Aria Group,[19] a wonderful flute player in New York. On one occasion, about two-thirds of the audience stood and applauded. Sam turned to me on stage and said, "I guess this is a crouching ovation, not really standing." So, we performers can feel whether it is heartfelt and merited.

The audience being supportive is particularly fitting. It describes accurately the audience's state of mind. An artist must have the support of the audience. An artist performs in part for the acknowledgment that the effort is valuable. We are like puppy dogs. We will do anything to be appreciated and loved.

Performing is certainly an experience where we expose ourselves; put ourselves at risk. Why do artists have stage fright? Because we go out there, first of all, not knowing if we will meet our own expectations, which we almost never do. And will the audience be pleased with what we do? Are they going to feel good about it?

A few years ago at Carnegie Hall, I heard a piano recital by the French pianist Pierre-Laurent Aimard. Among the pieces he performed was the Pierre Boulez Second Piano Sonata. About ten minutes into the performance, he stopped playing, stood up, looked at the audience of roughly 2,000 people and said, "If there is no silence, there is no music. Please be quiet. I shall start the piece again." I was shocked and yet, I admired his daring. The place was, no question, noisy. He made a forceful but unassailable demand, as he should, don't you think?

Yes, I agree, but—forgive me if I am a little critical—in some measure. Aimard was partially responsible for quieting the audience through the power of his playing. The audience is not entirely at fault; to win listeners over, the performer must play with sufficient intensity and commitment. A voice teacher with whom I studied once said, "You have to suspend the audience's coughing. You have to stop people from breathing when they're listening." So, to a large extent, audience reaction is the responsibility of the performer. If we play with enough commitment, we can stop the world from moving.

That is the power of a performer. So my response to audience disruption might be to blame myself. I would wish to focus with much, much more strength and dedication, and compel the listeners into silence, because the musical experience that is occurring on stage is important and unique and they should listen and never forget.

---

19   The Bach Aria Group is an ensemble, created in 1946, to perform the works of J. S. Bach.

In front of Metropolitan Opera doing my imitation of Beethoven on my way to my first recital at Tully Hall.

Chapter 5. The Proust Questionnaire

Daniel Pereira: *Bert, have you heard of the Proust Questionnaire?*

Humbert Lucarelli: Oh yes, I have heard of it, but can you explain it?

The Proust Questionnaire was a list of questions popular in the late nineteenth century in England and France. It was intended as a "confessional," to elicit insights about the respondent's personality. The novelist and essayist Marcel Proust completed the questionnaire while still in his teens. Proust's responses to the questionnaire were so whimsical and inventive—the manuscript of his answers was discovered in 1924, two years after his death—that the list came to be known as the Proust Questionnaire.

I would like to give you this Questionnaire. The questions are sometimes elemental, sometimes profound. Your answers should be no longer than one sentence, two at most. Shall we proceed?

Sure. I am happy to try it.

What do you regard as the lowest depth of misery?

I would say boredom.

Where would you like to live?

Where I am.

What is your idea of earthly happiness?

To be the fullest use of myself, for my friends and for my colleagues. When I say "use," I mean that I am fulfilling the moment.

What faults are to you the most indulgent?

Forgive my candor, but becoming depressed is very easy for me.

Who are your favorite heroes of fiction?

Okay; from Catcher in the Rye, Holden Caulfield.[20]

Who are your favorite characters in history?

Oh, perhaps because my perspective is as an American, I think first of those who have created this country. I would be fascinated to meet Benjamin Franklin and Thomas Jefferson and Alexander Hamilton and certainly, although not born in the United States, Albert Einstein.

Who are your favorite real-life heroines?

Oh, so many heroic women come to mind, some who are famous, some who are my friends, some who have accomplished so much, that they, literally, have changed the world. They continually humble me. You know, recollecting each one of them would take hours. But I look for people who

---

20   Taken from a J. D. Salinger novel.

have made positive and long-lasting contributions to their communities or to the world. Such as Eleanor Roosevelt who I actually met in the elevator at Roosevelt University when I was a student there. She was with Adlei Stevenson who she was nominating as the presidential candidate of the Democratic Party. There have been so many important women in my life who made a profound impact on me, like my sister. One of my most long time best friends, Sondra Myers, comes to mind. She has made an important contribution to my understanding perspective: what is important and what it is not, and she cares so much about people other than herself.

I'd rather not count the number of words there! What about your favorite painter?

Sorry, I'll try to be briefer, but some of these are big questions. Oh my God, so many names are possible. The Barnes Collection in Philadelphia particularly comes to mind. I saw such great Impressionist and post-Impressionist painters as Monet, Manet, Degas, Picasso and Renoir. What is so impressive about the painters there is not only their degree of accomplishment and truth, but also the variety of styles. I don't know why variety impresses me so much in painters. Selecting a favorite is impossible, because every artist speaks with his or her own voice. In music, it is the same.

If you think that question was difficult, wait for the next. Your favorite musician?

The one I am listening to at the moment. While I am listening to you play, you are my favorite. While I am listening to Arthur Rubinstein, he is my favorite; so, too Vladimir Horowitz, Jascha Heifetz, everyone. Again, the distinctions are impressive and charming. It is like food. I suppose the answer is: What I'm eating at the time is my favorite, as long as it has quality.

The quality you most admire in a man?

The ability to make good things happen, and the ability to change.

The quality you most admire in a woman?

The same.

Your favorite virtue?

Generosity of spirit. By that I mean not condemning, willingness, even eagerness, to accept others and the ideas of others.

Your favorite occupation.

Well, in a broad, philosophical sense, my favorite occupation is making something good happen. I love teaching, for sure, because teaching has the potential of making a more positive world. I also try to do that when I perform.

Who would you have liked to be?

I am pretty happy just being me. I am very lucky for my life and my friends. But I do admire certain qualities in other people. I especially admire individuals who are articulate. I am never articulate enough. I am invariably disappointed in myself when I can't successfully convey my point of view. So, articulating ideas is a dream, a wish. Maybe it would be nice to be Charlie Rose or maybe Oprah. They meet so many interesting people and have a great staff that does the research for them.

Your most marked characteristic?

Oh, okay. I think I have the quality of enlivening a gathering, walk into a room and energize it.

I can concur with that. What do you most value in friendship?

For that I must recall my grandmother's wisdom. She said that I should cherish friends who inspire me to dream of being more than I believe I can be.

Now, beware. What is your principal defect?

My principal defect? Well, I think I alluded to it earlier. That I am vulnerable, that I can collapse under negative pressure.

What would be the greatest of misfortunes?

Personally, it would be the loss of my friends.

What would you like to be?

I would like to be in a position to touch more people and to make everything and everyone around me better.

What is your favorite color?

I have two favorite colors. Well, several. Offering just one would be impossible. I like red, because it protects me. I like light blue, because it calms me. And I like Florentine red, dark, deep red, because it feels profound.

What is your favorite flower?

I like the deceptive simplicity of a daisy.

What is your favorite bird?

The duck. It quacks like an oboe.

Who are your favorite prose writers?

Oh, I admire Ursula Hegi,[21] who wrote Stones from the River. It speaks to the dignity and beauty of being different. I haven't read much fiction recently, so names don't immediately come to mind. I loved The Shipping News, by E. Annie Proulx.[22] It is a book that explores the possibility of change. It made me cry, and I had to stop while I was reading it. And, let

---

21 Ursula Hegi (b. 1946), German-born American writer.

22 Annie Proulx (b. 1935), American journalist and author, born in Norwich, Connecticut.

me not forget Joan Didion. She, like Metropolis, sets the bar too high.

Who are your favorite poets?

Well, I love everything from Shakespeare to Robert Frost, Maya Angelou. I love good quality. When I read it, it makes me feel good because I am enveloped in something important, not empty.

What are your favorite names?

I like uncommon names, unusual names. I was introduced recently to a woman whose name is Cyd. I thought that was terrific; an uncommon name, with a beautiful sound.

What is it you most dislike?

Period?

Period.

Negativity. It takes away and reduces the substance of what we are dealing with. It adds nothing.

What historical figures do you most despise?

I will be honest. Believing that evil exists is difficult for me. But certainly, when I think of someone like Hitler, I don't get it; people who are cruel, kill or torture. The audacity of killing is totally inconceivable to me, or the concept of inflicting pain to get what you want. Stupid.

What event in military history do you most admire?

There is no military history I can name because I am suspicious of military solutions; they force solutions that are not based on reason. The final result of a military resolution is resentment.

I admire peaceful revolution; peaceful change. Change can be accommodated, but it is never easy. It can also be painful, but it doesn't need to be. I don't think that change is necessarily painful, but it can bring about melancholy and sadness for what has been lost. So, the events in history that I most admire are those that brought change, naturally and profoundly. For instance, Nelson Mandela, who after being in prison for twenty-seven years, was liberated and became president of South Africa. He was a catalyst for peaceful change. It was not easy but, in the end, it was peaceful and remarkable.

Okay.

Yes, I hope that answers it.

Yes. Now let's go for the last four questions, which are, perhaps, the hardest. What natural gift would you most like to possess?

I guess the ability to make positive change.

How would you like to die?

Well, my father did it with dignity, peacefully, quietly, without excessive anguish, without pain, but most especially without doubt. Perhaps alone. Holding my sister's hand. He had no fear of death. A month before he died, he said to me with a twinkle in his eye, "I'm going to find out what is going on here before you do." And Ray Still had a good one. He died listening to the Saint Matthew Passion of Bach on earphones also while holding his daughter's hand. A great way to exit.

What is your present state of mind?

I am actually quite happy.

Last but not least, what, if you have one, is your motto?

To leave the world a better place than when I arrived. In some way, in any way, some small way, whatever I can do.

Wonderful.

That was tough.

Robert Bloom inscription, "To my dearest Bert With Love, Bob 1-18-77

Chapter 6. Learning

Daniel Pereira: *Tell me a little bit about your acting experiences. When did you do this, and how did it influence you?*

Humbert Lucarelli: I tried acting after completing my recording of Benjamin Britten's Six Metamorphoses. My interpretation on that initial recording seemed dull and uninteresting. Nothing was happening in the recording, no real dramatic expression. A critic said that I played very well at the concert before the recording, but that I was too self-effacing, that I wasn't coming to the audience enough. I had to figure out what to do, so I thought, "I'll try acting or painting or sculpture." Perhaps I could find the answer in a discipline outside of music.

Acting, and the whole idea of going into the audience, into the hall, is very important. In fact, my acting teacher taught me, as I walked onstage, to look at the far wall and sweep across the back of the theater with my eyes, to pull the theater inside my body; to pull the entire audience into me, as a way of acknowledging them. After that, I think, "Sometimes, while you're playing, you are here, sometimes you are there, sometimes you are in another place in the theater, or even outside the theater." You know what I mean? You can feel it; you're not always inside yourself.

Correct.

I don't know that anything is "always." I once asked my teacher Robert Bloom, "How much is here in your mind, and how much is in your heart?" He said to me, "100 percent in both places." I thought, "I only have 100 percent. Is it 50 and 50?" But I understand his meaning about 100 percent in both places. You're locked in and totally committed; nothing else exists when you perform.

Since we are on the subject of acting—and actors, musicians and dancers practice it—can you talk about your experience with Alexander Technique?

Yes. The idea of Alexander Technique shows me the path of letting go. It allows me to have the sensation of not controlling.

But does Alexander Technique not sometimes make you a little too aware of your body and of yourself? It could be counterproductive, in a certain way.

Yes, because it pulls you into your physical self. It pulls you here, it pulls you there. I love this idea, the feeling of the whole; the universal. Sometimes as I play, I take a breath. As I said, when I breathe, I inhale into my body all of the positive energy in the room. Then I put it back into the instrument. So, it is the idea of giving it back.

The Alexander Technique allows that to happen. Our bodies can be so tense for a number of understandable reasons and legitimate reasons. You know, the Alexander Technique returns you to the innocence of an infant. As we grow older and more experienced in the world, we develop fears, traumas. We begin to think too much. It would be so nice to be free of all that.

I am naïve. It is one of my flaws. But that creates a contradiction for me, to think of it as being a flaw, because as musicians we try to reach innocence. You want innocence and naïveté to go into the music, unencumbered by too many of your thoughts or feelings or sophistication. For sure, you have ideas about the music. In fact, the idea of playing in total obsequious "service to the composer" is a little bit flawed, because you cannot be in service to the composer if *you* don't exist. You must bring to the composer your vision of the piece.

One of my favorite thoughts, from the preface to a later edition of Thomas Mann's *Magic Mountain*, is about people who sent him doctoral theses analyzing his work. After reading their comments, he confessed that he had never thought some of those ideas. He said he would write to these people (which was so nice of him) and thanked them for "showing me to myself." As an artist, you hope that, when you play Scriabin, or whoever, that the composer, whether in heaven or hell, will say, "Thank you for showing me to myself." You showed him something about himself that he had not realized, or known, or appreciated. I hope the critics and my friends will sometimes do that for me.

Yes, absolutely.

You have a right—no, not a right but a responsibility—to take your position and your stand on every note you play. All performers must do this. A lot of performances today drive us crazy, because everybody's trying to be right. Everyone's trying to do what they think they are supposed to do, and they follow too many preconceived notions, instead of just allowing the music to happen; to come from inside. You have to find a balance. It seems a contradiction.

Yesterday I was listening to a re-mastered version of my recording of Hindemith, Poulenc and Saint-Saëns sonatas. Lyrichord Discs is reissuing them. I played the recording for a student who wanted to know what I think about them now. He said to me, "As you listen to this, would you like to change anything?" Good question! Several thoughts came to mind. It was recorded in 1968, when I was about thirty-five years old. Since then, I have coached and played these pieces many times. After talking about them so much and playing them so much, I have ideas now that didn't appear in these recordings. I would love to coach myself now. That would be fun.

The trouble with recording is that people who listen will say, "This is the way Bert plays this piece." And, of course, that's not the case. It's the way I played it *then*. It reminds me most of an old photo. You look at an old photo of yourself and you think, "Who was that?" It's the same thing. It's not that it's ugly or that it's not true, it's just what you were at that one moment.

This reminds me of Jorge Bolet, the Cuban-American pianist, who said that, after many years of performing a piece of music, studying it, playing it, restudying it, teaching it—you know, after a lifetime—the performer knows the piece even better than the composer. Do you agree?

Oh, yes, first of all because you experience the piece in front of an audience! If a composer had to stand on stage and in front of an audience, he might not write some things he wrote. I believe that's why Mozart and Beethoven and other composers who played their own pieces wrote with a sensibility that many of today's non-performing composers do not.

Absolutely.

My sheet music for the Strauss Concerto looks like the bottom of a birdcage; so many scratches and erasures and markings of thoughts and re-thoughts. I have countless ideas on interpreting a phrase. Last week with a student, I said, "Look at this passage. See how many ways you can play it, decide which of them (it may be not one, but several) you feel comfortable with. Play those. Then stop, and forget about it. Then, in front of the audience, don't try to make anything happen, just allow it to happen."

In a master class I once saw Julius Baker,[23] longtime principal flutist with the New York Philharmonic and Bach Aria Group, working with a student for twenty minutes, trying to perfect a phrase. He tried many possibilities. Finally, he said, "Look, do me a favor. Forget everything I said and just play it." It came out beautifully. The performance coalesced, because the student had explored all of the possibilities. Over the years, I have learned this about performance: There is clearly not just one way to do it.

What does the theatrical concept "breaking the fourth wall" mean to you as a musician? When and how did you learn about this?

The fourth wall is, of course, the wall between you and the audience. One of my first solo recordings was of the music of Benjamin Britten, the Phantasy Quartet and Six Metamorphoses after Ovid. I made it after a recital that I performed with funds from the Rockefeller Foundation. The recital's ticket revenues allowed me to produce the recording. As I said earlier, after I finished the recording and heard the final edit, I realized that the New York Times music critic who had said that I was a good oboe player, but too self-effacing, was correct.

I had to become more expressive; to communicate more effectively with an audience. I decided to look beyond music to develop these qualities, because, within music, I had been trained by two of the best, two very remarkable teachers. So, I thought, "Let me study painting, sculpting, and acting." I could explore the act of creativity in the field where I did not know so much about the craft. So, I worked with an acting coach from the Uta Hagen[24] school who taught me to, as you put it, break the fourth wall and *pull* the audience onstage with me. He taught me to acknowledge the audience.

---

23 Julius Baker (1915–2003), one of the foremost American orchestral flute players.

24 Uta Hagen (1919–2004), German-born American actress and drama teacher.

Taking the audience with you makes for a healthy and positive dynamic. These people have left their homes, paid money to be present in the hall, to have a good time and to hear you. It is a completely positive circumstance. Performers who don't deliver betray their audience. One of my teachers, Ray Still, once said, "You have to play in a way that makes the audience understand why they paid so much for their tickets."

The acting coach taught me technical things about being on stage, like walking onstage properly, finding and keeping the heat of the stage lighting on my face. Often musicians don't like lights shining in their eyes, because they are either reading music or too self-effacing. I had to learn to be comfortable with all of that.

Acting also taught me to listen. I don't listen enough in normal conversations. Acting taught me to listen to my colleagues. As I play with pianists, I hear everything they are doing, and in a chamber-music setting, I hear the other players. In the act of playing chamber music, my concentration must be more on the other players than on my own playing. My good friend, the flutist John Wion, whom I played with in The Lark Quintet, taught me that. The same is true of acting. Maybe the same is true of life.

When I studied sculpting, the teacher gave me a rock to work on. I said, "Well, what do I do with it?" He said, "Inside that rock is the sculpture that you want. Just take away what doesn't belong there." For me, this concept had a profound relationship to performing. The performance I dream of already exists. My responsibility is to remove the extraneous. In painting, I found I had the same problem that I was having as a musician: I was hanging on too much to the lines, to the craft, to the reality. I wasn't letting fantasy enter my mind. These were all important lessons to learn. It took time. It was not easy.

If I remember correctly, you spent some time in Mexico, dedicated entirely to practice. What motivated you to seclude yourself and practice in total isolation?

At a certain point in my playing career, in order to move forward, I felt I had to develop more facility, more strength as an instrumentalist and a closer relationship with my instrument. This required separating myself from my normal, day-to-day distracting environment. I remained in seclusion for four or five months. It was in a little town near Puebla de los Ángeles,[25] in Mexico where a friend of mine owned a house. She came on weekends and brought me food.

The house had neither electricity nor cooking facilities, so at night, I read by candlelight before sleeping, and I awakened at dawn with the sun. I practiced as many as six hours each day. The rest of the time I read books. That was an extraordinary time for me, because it placed stress on my embouchure, breathing and my mind. Pianists can practice much longer; twelve hours. The primary limitation for a pianist or a violinist is the ability to concentrate.

---

25   City located southeast of Mexico City.

We could talk about that!

Yes, I know what you mean by that, every instrument has its own problems, but playing a long time on a wind instrument brings its own peculiar physical challenges. The embouchure can't take it. Even slow practice is difficult. I did a lot of technical work, scales and the like. Upon my return to New York City, I was much stronger and I felt much more self-confident. In fact, it was a strange sensation. I don't know if you have ever experienced this. The instrument actually felt smaller. It really felt tiny to me. The instrument was no longer a foreign object. It became part of my body.

I heard Rostropovich, the cellist, play the premiere of a concerto at Carnegie Hall once by Henri Dutilleux.[26] It was an extensive work, approximately a twenty-seven-minute concerto. He played from memory, which is unusual; to take a new piece, memorize it and really master it. I went to the concert with the celebrated Russian cellist Raya Garbousova,[27] who taught with me at the Hartt School and became a good friend. Afterwards, she took me backstage to meet Rostropovich, and I asked him: "Maestro, how were you able to do this; this new work, completely memorized and flawless? How did you prepare?" He said, "Oh, I went to a little cabin in Canada, away from my life and I worked for six weeks only on this concerto." It takes a kind of madness to do such a thing, to make such a commitment, but that is what makes it interesting. Not too many people are so obsessed. This reminds me of the story about Fritz Kreisler, who, after a concert, encountered a young fan backstage who said to him: "Oh, Mr. Kreisler, if I could play like you I would give up my whole life." Kreisler replied, "Young man, I did." It is the only way.

People may envy your talent, but they pay money to hear you because you have been possessed to make effort that they would never make, would never want to make. And that's okay. You must have the discipline, the dedication, the love and the patience. You have to be nuts. You demonstrate a rarified level of playing that appears to be talent. It is not only talent; it is also working incredibly hard. At some point, you must take hold of yourself and do the work. I am not saying that talent does not exist, but it is such a smaller part of the whole product. Am I wrong?

No, you are absolutely correct. Sometimes, students seem not to care, nor to be willing to improve or grow. Have you ever lost faith in students or in yourself as a teacher and quit trying to help them?

No, for me, any relationship that fails will not come from my lack of patience or trying. I feel strongly about this. I can suffer the failure of a student, but I cannot suffer my failure as a teacher. That would be profoundly difficult to face. Once, I stood in front of a mirror, pointed at the image and said aloud, "You will not prevent me from realizing my dream." So, I keep struggling and keep trying and never stop searching for an answer. If the student gives up, I can say to him honestly, "It's okay if you want to give up. If you don't

---

26 Henri Dutilleux (1916–2013), French composer.
27 Raya Garbousova (1909–1997), Soviet-Russian cellist.

have the dedication or patience for it, it is fine. There is more to life than the oboe. There is more than music. The world is a big place where you can find your own element. But you must find something. You can't just float. Life is a casting director's dream. Casting yourself in the right role will bring you happiness and success. Casting yourself in the wrong role will be a disaster. Everyone can be happy and successful. You must just find the right setting to allow it to happen. You don't have to play the oboe." Steve Maxym who was a great bassoon teacher used to say to his students, "Only play the bassoon if you have to."

Confronting a subject is the most powerful means of working; to engage the subject without fear of failure. Successful people improve in any field because they can make falling short of their expectations a motivator to deepen their commitment.

Students have said to me that they began to love practicing after studying with me for a while, because I showed them how to practice. The techniques of expert practicing make them play better. That's important. Find your method of practicing and learning. We all have a different process. Some of us work slowly; some, quickly. Others repeat something over and over again. Some people need to back off of a problem and analyze it intellectually. Maybe we need to do all of them. Everybody is different. You must know yourself, be comfortable with yourself, be amused, enjoy it, and enjoy the process of being different. In spite of this, there are known ways of working efficiently. It is good to explore all of them and adapt them to your own specific needs. Wouldn't it be terrible if we were all the same? It would be like a science fiction book where everybody looks the same.

And yet, we are afraid of being different.

Each musician learns differently. Most important is that, onstage, you know what you are doing. When I say, "know," I don't mean to know only intellectually. I mean knowing. Your body knows, your psyche knows, your spirit knows. That's the fulfilling moment we all work for. It so rarely happens.

I read something interesting today suggesting that, to overcome the ego, we must think of everyone as we think of ourselves. And the ego will disappear. Often, I believe we see ourselves as distinct entities, but we are all the same. The more we believe that we are the same, the more quickly our egos will fade away.

The irony, of course, the contradiction is that we want to be different and, at the same, we want to be the same. We don't want to be different, because then we feel strange and alone. On the other hand, we must be different. This takes me back to Hegi's Stones in the River because it's about the privilege of being different. We have no choice. We just are. Each of us is a unique conglomeration of molecules. Just try to enjoy it.

Chapter 7. Teaching

Daniel Pereira: *Why is teaching important?*

Humbert Lucarelli: Teaching, has always struck me as a noble profession because it is fundamentally a means of passing on a tradition; it is a process of sharing between two human beings that supports the possibility of moving into a more positive future.

I have been lucky enough to have had teachers who were challenging, compassionate and stimulating, who gave me the audacity to believe that I was not trapped or frozen for life in a particular circumstance or condition; mentors who gave me the courage and support to believe that my capacity to grow and change was determined only by my own imagination.

Teaching is important to my life in music, because it embraces the act of self-discovery. Few of us can deal with the stark reality that the only meaningful answers come from within, and that when answers are harvested from the outside, the results are nothing more than a temporary solution to an issue only half understood.

Do you teach your students according to a particular system or a method that you have followed over the years?

I use no fixed system. I just work hard to respond to students, to what I hear them doing. Many good teachers keep a log of every lesson. Then, when a student comes back after a week, the teacher may say, "Okay, this is what we did last week, so now this is what we have to do next."

I could never teach according to a log, because I must work with the student walking in the door. That student may be a different musician and person than they were the week before. In a week's time, so much can occur to change a student. So, for example, I may be with a student who, ten minutes before the lesson, has been in a fight. That's going to change the whole dynamic of the lesson. Or, the student may not have had sufficient time to practice; or, conversely, too much time. As the teacher, I must adjust to the reality of the moment. I remember a student who, two days before her lesson, helped her father, who had incurable cancer, die. That was a lesson that neither one of us will ever forget.

Teaching is difficult because both the students and I must trust my instincts. Although I don't necessarily do this deliberately, I try to stay out of the way and let the lesson happen, just like in a performance.

I am blessed to have had such a variety of good teachers. Certainly my two principal teachers, Ray Still[28] and Robert Bloom, taught very differently. But lessons were profound, because they both worked within the moment.

---

28 Ray Still (1920–2014), American oboist who was principal with the Chicago Symphony for forty years.

During your career, and in your student years, did you follow a specific practice regimen in preparing for concerts or learning new pieces?

No, no particular regimen. I was never taught how to practice. I was lucky enough to have good instincts. Most important in my progress as a professional was my instinct to determine, almost invariably, the piece that was the most fitting for me to learn at each stage of my development. Not many musicians or students know what is best for them at a particular time. My students sometimes want to work on material that is too much for them—or too easy, that doesn't challenge them, or too difficult in ways that will hurt them. But that instinct of knowing what was the next best piece was one of the main attributes that helped me to grow.

I had a brief conversation once with the pianist Mollie Margulies, who was Rudolph Ganz's[29] assistant at the Chicago Musical College of Roosevelt University. She was in the College lobby looking frustrated, so I asked her, "Molly, what's wrong?" She screamed, "One of my freshman students insists on learning the Bach Goldberg Variations. That would be like giving Lobster Newburgh to a newborn infant. It would kill him!" Her response taught me a lot.

Another important factor in my learning process was my desperation to learn; my desire was so strong that I simply found a way to do it. One of my favorite Robert Bloom quotes was an answer that he gave to a young woman who asked him one time, after he played something beautifully, "Oh, Mr. Bloom, how did you do that?" He looked at her with an ironic smile, and said, "My dear, you have to want to do it very badly." I thought, you cannot want to do it very badly unless you know it exists.

That's why, a number of years ago, I asked you to develop a list[30] of important performers and performances that every student should know about. You need to know the possibility of great artistry. So, you can want it very badly. Remember, you can only want it if you know it exists.

People say that I never give up. I just keep going, because I believe. I believe in what I know. I've heard it, I know it is there. So I never stop. And I try to teach my students the process, the learning process. So many particular aspects of teaching continue to fascinate me and keep me engaged.

A good friend was at one time a terrific oboe player, having built an extensive career in Germany. But she halted her career in midstream to have a family. I was surprised by this sudden change, so I asked her, "What do you find so interesting about having babies, rather than oboe playing?" She said, "You know, it's watching them learn. It's just like what we do with the oboe. Watching myself learn, watching children learn; the whole process of learning is so phenomenally engaging."

My friend's comment made sense to me. We must support learning. Maybe our whole lives are about learning; how we learn, and our fears of being afraid of failing. We grow, we become fearful, we fall. We pick ourselves up,

---

29 Rudolph Ganz (1877-1972): Swiss pianist, conductor and composer.

30 See the list at the end of the book on p. xxx.

come back, and go a little further than before. Then it scares us, and we fall back again. This is the process. The learning curve is not a steady stream; it is a wave. When the practice seems not to be working, we must have the courage to persevere, because it will continue, it will come. But we must work at it and make the commitment. Commitment makes things work in the end.

But a minimum of talent must be present, or a certain basic capacity; physical, mental and emotional. Or do you believe that anyone can play anything?

Now you touch on a subject near and dear to my heart. I have been reading a book titled Talent is Overrated—giving it to students, and passing it around. The author Geoff Colvin claims, not that talent is nonexistent, but that it is certainly overrated. When we use a word like talent, we must ask, "What is talent"? Can you define it? I have my own definition of talent. If you find a better definition, call me collect. I will pay the bill.

For me, talent is nothing more than the ability to speak in a given medium. So, if you give the great violinist Itzhak Perlman an oboe, he shows no talent. He has no ability to play the oboe. Give me a violin, I, too, have no talent. If I give you a piano, you can play, you make it speak. When you play, you speak. That's what happens and people say you are talented.

That brings up another subject: When you speak, do you have anything to say? So, just as I mentioned a while ago that I am unable to believe in the concept of evil, I also cannot believe that someone is empty, that they have nothing to say. Some find it easier to access what they have to say; others find it more difficult, for a variety of reasons; emotional or psychological perhaps or maybe even physical. But everyone has something important inside. We must find the courage to allow it to emerge.

The confrontation with the instrument and with the arts has challenged me personally to go deeper inside myself. I couldn't have done this by any other means. I have said, half-jokingly, that intensive psychoanalysis might yield the same result. But music is so much better—to be with Bach and Mozart, Schumann, Schubert and Brahms—than lying on a couch, talking about yourself and weeping. I have gone to bed upset, because I was dissatisfied with a performance and myself. I am privileged to have had the opportunity of this confrontation with the oboe and music, and it wasn't by design. My father said, "Go play the oboe." At the time, I didn't even know what an oboe was!

So, when you say a minimum amount of talent, whatever that means, I don't know.

Well, in my experience as a teacher, I have come across students who seem incapable. They can't get it. They try hard; they fight, practice, repeat and follow all of my instructions. But they just can't get it…or it means I am a terrible teacher!

I know, I know, I know. Let me explain this. I don't believe that such students are untalented. I do believe that I have not discovered the key to helping them. I'll never forget one remarkable experience that I had as a teacher.

A girl who was playing the oboe solo from the Brahms Violin Concerto for me, sounded like she was reading a telephone book; nothing, no feeling. I had just seen the movie The Godfather. In one of its scenes, the uncle dances with his young niece with her feet firmly planted on his feet. At first she stumbles awkwardly; then she begins to feel the rhythm and the body motion. Finally, she just lets go and begins to dance with him.

So, I said to my student, "Do me a favor. Take your shoes off. Come over here and stand on my feet. Let's do a waltz, or a foxtrot. Just follow me." And so we danced. As we danced, we laughed, because we must have been a strange sight for anyone who happened to look in the window of door to the studio and see the two of us dancing around the room during an oboe lesson.

After about five minutes of dancing, I said to her, "Now, do me another favor. Pick up your oboe and play." She started to play, and I swear the change was remarkable. It was a transformation—phenomenal! Tears started streaming down her face. She said, "You know, we never touched in our family. I never hugged my father. I never touched a human being as we just did while we were dancing." Well, that was a wonderful breakthrough. Finding it was an accident. As teachers, we need to keep searching for the answer. I like to say that every artistic problem has 360 degrees. Just keep going around it until you will find the solution.

I must say that I learned as much from Robert Bloom's elbow as from any verbal instruction that he gave me because, as he was standing next to me urging me to play a phrase correctly, I could feel him lean into me I could feel the music in his body. In fact, he said to me, "If I could get inside your body and play the oboe, you would know what it felt like." It is the physical sensation of being expressive. Wow! It is a mystery. Ray Still once said to me practice everything with feeling. Your muscles need to learn the sensation of expression.

Russian pianists believed their so-called piano school, especially during the Soviet years, to be so efficient, that anyone studying within that system could become a great pianist. But that may not have been the reality. In fact, only the most talented children could advance, step by step, to the pinnacle: the Moscow Conservatory. Even at the local level teachers were very tough on their students and only a few managed to survive the rigors of the system. Merely hard work did not guarantee success.

Your comment is complex, because you have introduced several ideas. First, there is no system. The system lies within the individual student and teachers must go inside and find it. Your description is totally accurate and fitting: the "so-called" Russian piano school. I don't believe in schools of playing or teaching. The concept of schools of playing is fundamentally flawed, because it denies the individual. It says there is only one school that is valid one way to play. Art is a celebration of the individual.

As I have said earlier, after recently visiting Philadelphia's popular museum, the Barnes Collection, its holdings gather approximately fifty years of artistic endeavor, including such incomparable and unique artists as Picasso, Monet, Manet, Degas, Toulouse-Lautrec and Renoir, among others. The variety of artists and styles prevalent during those fifty years is mind-boggling. So, I think that the discovery of the self, who you are and what you have to say, is the most important part of the process.

Art is profound and wonderful because it helps you discover and accept the individual. And the struggle of the individual.

Schools and styles of playing are developed by individual oboe artists like Marcel Tabuteau, Robert Bloom, Ray Still, John Mack, Goosens, Lothar Koch and so many others to reflect or articulate their own personal aesthetic. An extroverted, flamboyant individual will develop a playing technique that serves an extroverted aesthetic or style. A conservative, introspective artist will develop a technique that will manifest his introspection. Artists must discover their own aesthetic, their own heart, their own interior, and develop a technique that will accommodate that. The resulting technique can be called a school of playing. But it comes from the individual. Schools come from the followers. Not the creators.

So, my next question is: Why do you teach in a school?

Now I think you are talking about an institution, not a way of playing. The institution of a music school serves a very important function. I have recently retired after teaching forty-five years at The Hartt School at The University of Hartford. I went to school at Chicago Musical College, now the Chicago College of Performing Arts at Roosevelt University, students were brought together, who could share the pain of learning; and also because we all need some sort of structure in our lives, logistically, and humanly, as well as the financially. It is also well known that musicians and artists function most effectively in a structured environment.

This year, the President of Roosevelt University, Charles Middleton, where I went to school, is retiring. The school has a brilliant history that has been documented by The University Historian Lynn Weiner in a book, *Roosevelt University (Campus History)*. Chuck has added to that history in a very profound sense. He, in my mind, has been the ideal university president and has set a very high bar for all university presidents everywhere. He brings to his job an incredible balance of fundraising, vision and humanism that sets him apart.

It is a pity that the term "music school" seems an oxymoron. It is a systemic problem. Those two words do not even belong together in the same sentence, because music is in service to the individual. Institutions, schools need to suppress the individual out of systemic necessity. An orchestral musician who feels the need to skip a rehearsal in order to make reeds cannot do so. Rehearsals must be the priority, because forty other musicians depend on every player to be on hand. Everyone has to be together. That illustration is simplistic, but, in an institution, we are all part of a larger structure. We must serve that structure first.

A classic example. In my last year at Roosevelt University, I had a scheduling professional conflict with a dress rehearsal that was scheduled for the school orchestra. I didn't ask to be excused—not the wisest choice. I decided instead, "Oh, I'm going to be absent. I have to do it." It was, "Don't ask, and don't tell." And so I didn't attend the rehearsal. For missing that one rehearsal, the conductor decided to fail me in orchestra for the entire semester. I would not be able to graduate, for lack of a single orchestra credit.

The reason I missed this rehearsal was because, at that exact same time, I was playing with the Chicago Symphony. The school orchestra director preferred to stop me from graduating, rather than support a student player's professional success. That's insane. I complained to the dean. He said, "Oh, we'll work it out." He did. I got my credit and graduated.

Extraordinary situations arise requiring a player, as in this example, to miss rehearsals or other school obligations. Such conflicts of interest disadvantage the school groups and the other players who need all members of the ensemble to be on hand. In the end, the school administration must decide on a case-to-case basis, but the conflicts are often irresolvable. Does that make any sense?

So, we must try to satisfy both sets of expectations. It's just not easy. I didn't really learn to play the oboe until after leaving school. In some respects, school placed a lid on my ability to master my craft effectively, because I was just learning the required repertoire in any way I could: by the *seat of my pants*. I had to play a certain piece on a Wednesday—to go in and know the passage of the music whether I played it well or badly, I had to do it, to get to the end of the piece. That's not true learning. That's not true discovery. That's survival.

I have the impression that universities sometimes behave like corporations, like businesses. It has happened that students who are awarded degrees don't deserve them. Degrees are granted because the university is forced to show a satisfactory graduation rate. The university needs "customers." If the curriculum is too rigorous, students will not attend the school.

Yes, some schools operate like this, and some do not. The problem is systemic.

The book I mentioned earlier, *Talent Is Overrated*, is particularly valuable, because the author, a senior editor at *Fortune Magazine*, approaches the concept of talent from the vantage points of business, music and sports, and then shows their similarities. The world of business and the world of sports as well as the actual act of making music hold many attributes in common.

Music schools have become overly institutionalized. It doesn't work so well. And yet we must operate within the framework of an institution, in order to compare ourselves to colleagues who surround us there, and as I have said, "to share the pain of learning."

Even if the level is substandard?

Basic performance and intellectual standards are essential. Let's not forget that schools are ranked by independent organizations. To understand the relative value of a degree, we clearly need to take into account the ranking of the school from which the degree is granted as well as the public perception.

Attending a university has its advantages, but education there is generally uniform. In spite of the fact that some students need specific training while others may not, all unfortunately receive the same standard education.

So, at what point does standardization become little more than setting benchmarks? To me, this concludes the discussion of the advantages and disadvantages of schools. Negotiating these troubled waters requires a clever and sensitive administration, as well as intelligent and savvy students.

Right now after forty-five years I have retired from The Hartt School of The University of Hartford in West Hartford, Connecticut and continue teaching at New York University. There is in our music department another brilliant and balanced person as the Director of Double Reeds. His name is Matt Sullivan. He brings to his job the same qualities as Chuck Middleton. He has a vision for the school that balances Fine Arts with the best of a Music Conservatory environment, making NYU at the forefront of the future of music schools.

As a teacher, do you subscribe to the necessity of reaching to the student at a deeper level of acquaintance, including addressing personal or private problems? For the purpose of the lesson or for the sake of the music, should the teacher connect personally with the student or is mixing the professional and the personal completely unnecessary?

You have to know what the student is thinking and feeling. If I trust myself, I will most often get it right. Not trusting myself, and being insensitive to a student or insensitive to the person in the room aggravate me. It is what disappoints me the most about myself: when I miss it. I need to say the right thing at the right time in order to have an impact. I can offer an idea at the wrong moment, and it means nothing. If I find the right moment, it will change the student's life!

I tell students that you can't do anything in life, whether a phrase, or a tone color, or a rhythmical nuance, without conceptualizing it first. I once was teaching a bassoon student who was having trouble playing in tune. So, first I tried the simplest idea I played the note on the piano. Then I said, "Now, play that note, but before you play, listen to it and imagine what it sounds like when you play it." Following that instruction, he played perfectly in tune. You have to conceptualize it first. That's all part of the process.

Probably no other country in the world has as many conservatories, colleges and universities with music departments as the United States. Many are among the best in the world. Still concerns remain about the quality and efficiency of the teaching methods and systems applied in these schools. How would you change—or improve—the approach of these schools to teaching music effectively?

American music schools today produce players with tremendous facility. They have remarkable control; they can play much better than those who have gone before. I hear young players now; unbelievable what they can do. Playing as I did fifty years ago, when I first started, I wouldn't have a chance against these kids today. They are very accomplished.

They are accomplished technically, but the artistry is always rare today. You remember, someone said to the violinist Fritz Kreisler, while they were judging a competition: "Isn't it wonderful that the playing has improved so much and grown over the years?" Kreisler replied, "Oh, yes, the level of mediocrity is much higher now."

Oh, sadly true.

So, to rise above mediocrity, you must find what is inside, but teaching this in a school is difficult on many levels.

Maybe the job of a college administrator is to understand that exceptions are common, they are not the exception. Being an administrator is easy if you blindly follow established rules. Actually, you don't even need an administrator. You just need a computer to say, "These are the rules. No exceptions." But the human element must enter the process. That is the point. Too many music schools miss the human element. They don't have sensitive administrators who can look more closely, find the real problems and determine the best resolutions.

Being a good music school dean is like being an artistic "zoo-keeper." You have to make every student and faculty member feel indispensable and irreplaceable to the future of the school. It is actually a worse job than being an oboe soloist.

Very true. My next question is simple. If you had one word—and only one word (I know this is hard)—to tell young musicians what they need to do to grow and succeed, what is that one word?

Stubborn. Never give up.

I knew it!

You knew I was going to say that?

I had no doubts!

You must never take "no" for an answer. I love everyone who has said "yes" to me, because they have helped me to believe in myself and become all that I am today. I also love everyone who has said "no" to me because they challenge me to work harder.

How do you teach a student to play a musical phrase? And what are the basic points within a musical sentence?

You remember I told you to make a list of fifty performers everyone should listen to on YouTube. YouTube is free; there is no excuse not to listen.

Again, my grandmother said, "You become what you eat." You did the list, and you even included me on it. I don't know, I don't think I deserve to be on such a list. However, a copy of the list needs to be included in this conversation. Of course, I teach the technical operation of a phrase. Whether a crescendo or diminuendo and to what degree; whether you have some place to go; finding the high point and its relation to the resolution. It is like the structure of a sentence: Where is the comma, where is the period? But, most importantly, the phrase has to speak, to say something.

I urge students to play a phrase as speech, telling a story, and, most important, recognizing the vowel sounds in the notes, understanding that some notes—the Italian vocals are "ah," "eh," "ee," "oh," "oo,"—basic vowel sounds. In the Brahms Violin Concerto, for example, if I sing a different vowel on each note, it begins to sound like speaking.

So, perhaps anyone, no matter the country or language, might sing the same vowels on the same notes. Those vowels seem natural to those notes in that line—so illustrating, in one sense, what seems the universal musical language. Even certain consonants seem to be natural. I hum a vowel and put "m" on the end of every note. It is like tapering a note with a diminuendo.

I work on all these ideas with students, and try to get them to speak and say something that is musically meaningful. Becoming confident that they have something to say is a challenge for many students. Often, they don't speak, they don't express, because they are shy or assume they are wrong. They don't have the courage to be wrong.

Or they don't know what to say.

Yes, they don't know what to say. So I try to convince them: What you say doesn't matter, as long as you say something. It is all non-verbal anyway. Once, playing a Telemann piece, I imagined a story about a little boy walking his dog and the dog pulling on the leash; so, the push and pull of the boy and his dog. It was simplistic, but it told a story, a little back-story. Listeners will imagine their own stories if the player is saying something. That is the wonder of the abstraction of music. The non-verbal component is universal, and we all bring our own interpretation to it.

Some aspects of music are fundamental. Some pieces of music may make you cry, others stimulate happiness or distress. There are different levels and textures to happiness and sadness. Those emotional reactions are basic. Does that begin to answer your question?

Certainly. What is a true legato, and how do you achieve it?

What is a true legato? Good question. Well, a legato is a way of moving from one note to another, but doing it well is elusive. In some cases, another word used is portamento. It means connecting notes so that they flow into one another, almost like lava. You can feel the connection. Some like to think of it as honey or even mercury. These are all textural connections that a player could make. Molasses is different from honey, and honey is different from water. And so, you try to connect.

You can even play a legato with rests between notes; those isolated notes can connect. Brahms specifically asks for this. He writes a note with a rest and a legato marking over it. For me, hearing a pianist who can create a legato is astonishing; totally magic.

Like the Brazilian Guiomar Novaes? [31]

Ah! You remember! Yes. Guiomar Novaes performing the Schumann piano concerto. Making a legato on the piano is virtually impossible, because every note played has a diminuendo, a decay. Not only can you not do a crescendo from one note to the next, but you can't really connect. So, how to keep the sound moving from one note to the next? Every good pianist confronts this enigma and resolves it. One way to resolve it is, as the first note decays, you bring the next note at the exact right moment. So you pick notes up one after the other and create a forward motion. You don't let a note really die. And, even if you do, with legato, the connection is in the mind and the ear. It's in the imagination. Between the notes is energy, and you can hear it.

As you edit a recording, you don't listen just for the silence between the notes. You feel the energy between two notes that are not physically connected. Hearing that organic connection challenges the ear and the mind. It shows the power of your imagination over the sound. Does that make any sense?

It does.

Yes, to keep it going, all the time, you must not let notes die.

It's truly unusual, isn't it?

Yeah. Oh, yeah. Oh, I just created a legato with my words! I said, "Yeah...Oh yeah, oh yeah." I could keep that going for a long time. I didn't say, "Yeah. Oh yeah. Oh, yeah." There's a drop between each one of those words, you see? You do the same when you play.

Yeah...Oh yeah.

Playing a phrase, I make a particular expressive statement. Then the next phrase is connected, but it repeats. It is a reiteration. Or it can say, "Well, on the other hand, here is a different idea." Or if you repeat the same phrase several times over you need to let me know the last time you play it that you are going to go on. Otherwise, going on does not make sense. It's pointless, unless you're trying to surprise the audience, which in itself can be gratuitous and also sort of pointless. Does that make sense? That shows interpretive options; the ability to show your listeners the variety and latitude of the phrase's expressive potential. You try to illuminate your

---

31 Guiomar Novaes (1895–1979), Brazilian pianist.

take on the composer's wishes, but you never know if you are correct or if you have imposed on it with your own imagination. In a great piece and a great composer, you can always find room for your imagination. You are not required to say unerringly what the composer would have said. First of all, you don't really know. But it has to be thoughtful not arbitrary.

As I have said before, in the preface to the second edition of *The Magic Mountain*, Thomas Mann explains that many scholars, who have written about the book, send him their work. He replies, with pleasure I think, "What you're saying is not wrong, but it is not what I was thinking. Thank you so much for showing me to myself." Thomas Mann is a powerful example of an artist who is secure.

A frequent issue that musicians face is the necessity of concealing the bar line. Has this ever been a problem for you as a performer? And how do you help your students with this challenge?

Forgive me. I must bring the metronome into the conversation. The metronome is the musician's best friend. It is the pulse. Every living creature has a pulse. The bar line gives structure to the pulse, just as in poetry. It can be in three; one-two-three, one-two-three. But a strong beat needn't always occur on "one." It can be one-TWO-three, one-two-THREE, one-TWO-three, ONE-two-three, etc. But you always need to know where the beginning of the measure is.

So the variety that you give to the pulse within the bar is necessary, interesting and expressive. It helps the listener feel his body moving. I say "moving," but do I mean moving physically, or moving in an emotional sense? Each beat of the bar is different.

I insist that my students count one measure before they begin; they invariably come in on the correct beat of the measure. You can't just play out of context because it has no structure. You lose the form and function.

If a piece starts on two, then you must hear it as two. You can't start two as if it were one, unless you have some underlying expressive purpose. That would be a conscious decision; poetic license. But normally, if the entrance is on three or four; three or four is an upbeat: four-one, or three-one. The last beat of a measure is a preparation for the beginning of the next measure.

Theodore Reik was a student of Freud. In his book *The Symbols of Man* he compiled and explained symbols that are universal in all civilizations. He discovered that one of the most powerful symbols is the number three. It is found in so many forms—the Holy Trinity, the pyramids—he had a whole list. Perhaps the most difficult relationship to sustain is among three people. Two will always come upon a connection better than the other two, or maybe it even varies by the moment. Three is a kind of structure. It is the positioning of exposition, development and recapitulation. It is ubiquitous. It is everywhere.

Numerology and its relationship to art is an imperative and fascinating subject. The universal character of the number three and its importance are especially evident in the area of harmony. The fundamental chords are

I [tonic], IV [subdominant], V [dominant], and then the resolution back to I. It is still a harmonic structure of three: I, IV and V.

You can also extend some of these individual harmonic structures. You can do *one, four, five*. Or *one, foooouuuur, five*. Or *one, four, fiiiiiiiiiiive*. The phrase becomes elasticized. Musicians who do this as they play magically create an internal tension in the line with creative variety.

My teacher Robert Bloom invariably played a phrase with subtle pauses at important moments. It was only subliminally perceptible to the listener. The line appeared to be moving continuously. How he did that always amazed me.

The measure of an artist is mastering the essential silence, but still maintaining the line. The silence is part of the music. The same holds true in conversation.

If you say, "(pause)…as I just did." You pause. The art lies in mastering the pause between the notes, but still keeping the audience moving with the line.

It is considered that John Cage's 4'33" was such an original, inventive idea. Recently, I read a book[32] written by the twentieth-century writer and musicologist Boris de Schlözer, who was Alexander Scriabin's brother-in-law, and also his student. De Schlözer, who was also a philosopher and amateur physician, reported Scriabin to have told him that a piece of music would one day be written consisting entirely of silence, nothing else. This conversation took place some forty years before 4'33".

Fascinating. In conversation with a colleague at The Hartt School I said once, during a rehearsal, "You know, that silence was out of tune." He went into hysterics. He understood, of course, that the last note played, before moving on, must relate to the next. Or the silence could be too loud. Or it could be too soft. I am continually fascinated with speaking gestures. I say, "Yeah, yeah," then I stop. Because, to me, silence means that the speaker is thinking. The most interesting people are thoughtful conversationalists. They think before they speak—not just what they say, but how they say it. That's an important quality. Maybe even essential to music, don't you think?

Yes, it is better to speak mindfully than the other way around.

You see this mistake most often by some politicians who talk before their ideas are formulated. They are mindless. They often say what they think they should be saying Some musicians play mindlessly and also without feeling. Why do performers play without feeling? Do they have no feeling? I doubt it. They play without feeling, because they fear being wrong. They fear exposing their vulnerability. I suppose some politicians are the same. Maybe we all are.

I love music, because the expression is non-verbal. In the act of playing, you must simply show that you feel. Recently, you remember that I referred to an

---

32 Boris de Schlözer (1881–1969).

article in an issue of Lapham's Quarterly magazine on communication,[33] in which the author said that understanding an actor's words was not essential, because he took in as much meaning from vocal intonation and physical gesture as he did from the words themselves. I think we were talking about this in relationship to subtitles in opera performances. The essence of non-verbal communication is an important topic of discussion for musicians, especially singers. Sometimes, there can be a creative tension between the meaning of the words and the meaning of the gesture.

Even in opera, as I said before there is a controversy surrounding the supertitles that are projected above the stage or on the seat in front of the spectator regarding whether they benefit or distract the audience. The notion of attending an opera only to read the libretto while it is being sung is bizarre. Why would a concertgoer pay $250 for a ticket to read a libretto during the performance? The spectator is neither listening nor watching. He is reading! The singer's expert placement of the sound, not the words, moves the listener. True enough, the meaning of the words affects the performer's and the listener's perceptions of the moment. But if they are both really engaged, the sound and music will reflect the meaning.

As I also mentioned earlier, I heard the French National Theater during its tour in New York. Although I didn't understand much of what was being recited, it was still very moving and touching. At times, I cried and at times I laughed. It was like music: perfect. I loved that whole experience.

Moving to another subject now, if you had to design a workout sheet, a list for a young student—scales, etudes, pieces, sight-reading exercises—for regular, daily practice, what kind of program or diet would you recommend?

That's easy. First, I like the book known as the Barret Book, written by Apollon Marie-Rose Barret,[34] who was principal oboist of the Italian Opera in London for many years during the late 1800s. This book not only has many challenging technical etudes, but it has forty melodies that help the student develop musical phrasing. I suppose the reason I like it so much is that it was the first book that has an important impact on my playing. I also recommend the Method for Oboe by Joseph Sellner, which is an excellent book of exercises and etudes. There are many good etude books. The challenge is to find one that is musical. Why would you want to practice technique using non-musical material?

In the preface of another excellent etude book, written by Georges Gillet, there are some valuable comments on effective practice. Gillet recommends no more than three hours per day of practice. The fourth hour is almost not worth the trouble. Of course, with the oboe there could be another hour or two of reed making.

I recently saw a quote of Leopold Auer where he said, regarding the amount of time a student should practice, "Three hours if they are good, four hours if they are a bit stupid, and if they need more than four, they

---

33   Lapham's Quarterly magazine.Volume V, Number 2, Spring 2012.

34   Apollon Marie-Rose Barret (1804—1879), French oboist and professor at the Royal Academy of Music in London.

should try another profession." Nice anecdote but seems a bit harsh to me. Some people take more time than others. This is not a horse race. I have seen some composers write very fast and some agonize over every note. Instrumentalists are the same. I have known players who learn the notes very fast but never learn the music.

Gillet recommends practicing scales for one hour, etudes for one hour, and then repertoire for one hour, which is fine unless you are working on a recital. But you must be careful. If you are preparing for a recital, you might fall into the trap of working only on the recital repertoire. Even before a recital, you must continue to practice some scales, to keep the oil in your joints working and your ears listening. So, still, scales, etudes, and then repertoire.

Repertoire is a thorny subject for oboists because within the standard classical canon, music for solo oboists is quite limited. We have no Beethoven concerto. We have only one Mozart. No Schumann concerto. No Brahms. So much is missing. We must find alternatives. Just the exercise of building a recital is a challenging one for an oboist.

A performing artist is not a credible soloist unless they play concertos. You must do some concerto work. Just as singers, typically, are not quite validated without some opera in their experience. You can do a little. You can keep it to a dull roar. But you must do some. So, instrumental soloists must play at least some concertos.

So, what concertos do we oboists have to play that are written by historically well-known composers? We have Mozart, Strauss, and Vaughan Williams. From there, we get into trouble. We have only three, maybe four— Martinu. But managers booking you for a concert don't want the Martinu concerto. They say, "What is that? I can't sell that." I told one once, "People sell cigarettes that cause cancer and you can't sell Martinu?"

I have played the Mozart Quartet for Oboe and String Trio many, many times. Once, a manager asked me to do it, but I said, "Can't you find me something else to play? I have done that so often." His reply taught me a lot. He said, "You know, my audience has never heard the Mozart Oboe Quartet played live. It would be so wonderful if you could do that for them." Well, honestly, hearing that broke my heart. So I said to him immediately, "Oh, absolutely. No problem, I will do it." We musicians want to play music that is new to us, not remembering that even some of the most traditional works that are old chestnuts to us are new to the audience.

Absolutely. That happened to the pianist Van Cliburn. After winning the Tchaikovsky Competition in Russia, he played little else but the Tchaikovsky and Rachmaninoff Concertos.

Exactly. He did that for maybe three years. I don't think he played anything else. But, you know, they were paying him for the Tchaikovsky. Audiences wanted to relive that experience of winning the competition with him. I understand that. I hope he understood it, too. Later, after several years, he played other concertos beautifully, including the Schumann Piano Concerto.

Yes, his recording of it is marvelous.

Yes, beautiful. He did try to enlarge his repertoire. But in the end, people still wanted to hear the Tchaikovsky. It's the piece with which he won the competition.

Since we are talking about competitions, many well-known musicians have criticized them and their detrimental effect on the young artists who compete. Did you ever participate in competitions? Are you an advocate or opponent of them?

I was never a competition player. During my student years, oboe competitions were rare. Later, however, I organized three international competitions. A bequest from a woman who died of cancer funded the first one. She believed in me—trusted me—so she left me $60,000. The money didn't belong to me; it did speak to her insight about my musicianship and the value that she placed on it, but I felt a responsibility to use her gift to do something positive for music.

So, I established a competition. The team who helped me launch it said that associating my name with the competition would add to his credibility. So we called it the "Lucarelli International Competition for Solo Oboe Playing." We held two more, but I was uncomfortable with my name in the title. So we changed it to the "New York International Competition for Solo Oboe Playing." President of the Juilliard School, Joseph Polisi generously and graciously gave us the Juilliard Theatre for the finals and only charged for the cost of keeping the theater open. He is a man who knows how to nurture the arts.

At the awards ceremony after the finals at The Juilliard School I told the competitors: "The most valuable part of a competition is its deadline. It gives you a wall to knock down, a goal for your practice." Practicing in a vacuum without concerts to prepare for is difficult. For that purpose, a competition has value. It gives musicians a hurdle to leap over.

Musicians with successful careers are not necessarily competition winners. Winning a competition doesn't guarantee a career—and certainly not just one competition. How many Van Cliburn Competition winners can you name? As a professional pianist you certainly know more than most, but not that many come to my mind. I remember Andre-Michel Schub[35] as a Cliburn winner, because I worked with him. I don't recall any other winners. A successful career comes from your intensity, your passion, your love, your commitment and certainly your ability to build an audience. Most important to sustaining a career is building an audience. It's similar to a presidential campaign; attracting constituents, persuading listeners to trust you and your ability to touch them.

As a performing artist some organize festivals and engage other musicians. In a sense, it makes one influential. Your real purpose needs to be not so much to become influential, but to find a way to contribute something

---

35 Andre-Michel Schub (b. 1952), French pianist, winner of the Gold Medal at the 1981 Van Cliburn International Competition.

positive. If the gesture is merely self-aggrandizing, it will fail. Your growing influence needs to be an added side value for your career.

If you have a good manager, it could be helpful. Their roster of artists becomes part of your focus. Sometimes managers capitalize on their rosters and sometimes they don't. A manager with credibility can pick up a telephone, call someone and say: "This is a substantial artist. Believe me. You should engage this person." Managers with this sort of credibility are important but rare.

Chapter 8. On Repertoire

Autographed Pencil Manuscript *short score* of Strauss Oboe Concerto showing important differences from what is published, with two autographed photos

Daniel Pereira: *One of the most important masterpieces ever written for the oboe is the Richard Strauss concerto, which you have played many times and recorded as well. What is your vision of this remarkable and challenging piece?*

Humbert Lucarelli: Yes this recording is, I think not so bad or as the French might say is "pas mal". The Lehigh Valley Chamber Orchestra with its conductor Donald Spieth gave, in many ways a generous collaboration. Donald Spieth is one of those unusual musicians who knows how to deftly walk the dangerously thin line between leading and following that can result in magic. It was a joy to work with him.

In fact one of the proudest moments of my career is on this CD. The First movement of the Vaughn Williams Concerto, is in a single take.

You are correct about the Strauss. It is challenging technically, tonally and in physical endurance as well. It's a twenty-four- or twenty-five-minute work. In the first two pages, the oboe plays continuously. Playing ceaselessly on the oboe because of the embouchure and breath is very difficult. The digital requirement of this concerto is also demanding. Another aspect is equally important: What is the piece doing? What is it saying?

The Oboe Concerto is one of Strauss's last works; it seems to be without form. Some critics say the piece rambles, but they miss the point. It is exactly what it is, an old man looking back and talking about his life just rambling all over the place. Before the Oboe Concerto, Strauss had written *Die Frau ohne Schatten*, an opera that took chromaticism to the edge; it's almost twelve-tone. After Strauss' *Die Frau*, Arnold Schönberg could only go to one place: twelve-tone music. That's an interesting period in the history of Western Music, when composers were experimenting a lot. On the other hand, the Oboe Concerto is very retro. It's a typical and charming thing about us as we get older.

Being in the "autumn" of his life, Strauss identifies with the Marschallin who feels she has lost her charm and beauty when the power to attract has passed. The concerto even seems to contain quotes from *Der Rosenavalier*, including waltzes, as well as the autobiographical *Ein Heldenleben*. In the end, the Oboe Concerto strikes me as the real autobiographical *Ein Heldenleben*, translated as "A Hero's Life."

The sentiment in the second movement of the concerto is similar to the moment when the character of the Marschallin grieves in *Der Rosenkavalier* at the end of act one, and in the famous trio at the close of the opera, at, which point she contemplates the passing of time. One has the distinct feeling in this concerto that Strauss is saying this musically to himself, as he takes Hugo von Hofmannsthal's libretto —I paraphrase, "All things earthly are but empty dreams. All things must pass. And there is a time at first, when *time* feels like nothing, and there is a time when we think of nothing else. Our souls are filled with the thought of the passing of time. This is a truth that I am speaking to myself." She says, "I am at the end."

Just before the cadenza in the concerto there is a deeply personal utterance, introduced by the horns. For me, this is the most beautiful moment in the concerto. In the opera you can hear the despondent feeling of resignation. Anger and disappointment would never be allowed to be shown by a woman the stature of the Marschallin.

But now in the cadenza of the concerto there is also anger and frustration expressed. This is Strauss' concerto. This is Strauss' frustration. He can say what he wants. It is his utterance. Listen to what he is saying...
And then Strauss follows all of this at the end of the cadenza with a metamorphosis of descending chromatic trills taking us out of his anger with a flourishing two-octave D-major scale that thrusts us into the last movement of joyful music remembering his last librettist, Stefan Zweig, who committed suicide saying, "Let us meet our fate with lightness. Life punishes those who do not do so."

What a great moment!

Shall we continue with other landmark works in the oboe repertoire? John Corigliano's Oboe Concerto, for example, written for you and which you premiered at Carnegie Hall in 1975 with Kazuyoshi Akiyama[36] conducting the American

---

36 Kazuyoshi Akiyama (b. 1941), Japanese conductor.

Symphony Orchestra, and then recorded for RCA Victor. What was your connection to Corigliano at the time, and could you describe the concerto in terms of oboe playing and musical ideas?

John and I were friends. In fact, before he wrote the concerto, I found an apartment for him in my building. I had just begun doing solo work and had made public my intention to become a soloist, having performed three recitals at Alice Tully Hall in the 1973 concert season.

The New York Arts Council had established a program to commission concertos for well-known performers. At the time, Arthur Bloom was the assistant to Leonard Altman, the Arts Council's director. Art, who was also the clarinetist in my quintet, called me one day and said, "Hey, you are doing a lot of solo stuff, and we just got this new program to commission concertos. Would you like to commission a concerto for the oboe?" I replied, "Yes, of course." So he said, "Well, find somebody who you think would write a great piece."

I looked around and settled on John. He was a friend, and he had already begun to do some important composing. He was a committed musician and a natural choice. For twenty-five years, his father was concertmaster of the New York Philharmonic. He had excellent training and had been around music his entire life. John knew what great music-making and music were. He was also at the beginning of his career and stood to benefit from a commission of this magnitude. I could trust that he would take it seriously.

So I asked him to do it, and he responded by taking oboe lessons from me before starting to write. He asked me to get him an oboe, and I gave him lessons for three or four months. This shows you exactly what he is; conscientious is a word I would use to describe everything John does. He said to me, "I want to write a concerto that is really an oboe concerto. It won't be a concerto that can be played on a clarinet or flute or any other instrument." He said, "It must really be an oboe concerto that captures the character of the instrument and its possibilities."

The concerto's first movement is called "Tuning Game," because the oboe tunes the orchestra. In fact, at the premiere I began by playing with my back to the audience, tuning the orchestra only after the piece had started did the audience didn't know what was going on.

The second movement is called "Song," because John said, "The oboe sings, so let's do that." For the third movement, "Scherzo," I suggested that he incorporate contemporary techniques that were coming into fashion at that time with the oboe—multiphonics, almost chord-like sounds, high notes and extended techniques, such as flutter-tonguing. He wrote this movement just for oboe, harp, piano and percussion. It is really very effective.

The fourth movement is an "Aria," but turned upside down, because, he said, "The oboe has a big, fat sound in the low register. So, let's make this aria upside down, and it will reach its 'high point' in the low register." This is exactly the kind of thoughtful, innovative thinking that is so creative and interesting about John's writing. This movement has a big cadenza that is very much like violin writing. He dedicated it to his father.

The last movement is called "Rheita Dance." The year before, John had been on vacation in Morocco, where he heard the rheita, a Moroccan folk instrument that is similar to an oboe. It is a conical bored, double-reed instrument, but played with the reed completely inside the player's mouth. It's almost like a shawm, a Renaissance instrument. It makes a coarse, ugly sound, because the reed is not controlled by the embouchure. This movement is a wild, frenzied dance inspired by the sound of the Moroccan instrument. This is the movement we spoke about earlier.

So that is the piece. It has now become a staple in the oboe repertoire. *The New York Times* cited this recording on RCA Victor Records as one of the twenty-five best recordings of twentieth-century music since World War II. I am proud of being a part of that honor. The project helped to put both John and me on the map. In fact, he generously autographed my copy of the manuscript, "For Bert, who started it all. With admiration and love."

Concerto for Oboe, microfiche of Movement III Scherzo,
inscribed "For Bert – Who started it all! With admiration and love, from John Corigliano, 1994"

Shall we talk about the Canzonetta for Oboe and Strings by Samuel Barber, which you recorded with the Lehigh Valley Orchestra? Among your recordings, it is one of my favorites. You knew Barber personally, correct?

Well, I met Barber a few times. We were not friends but certainly we were casual acquaintances. Originally, the Canzonetta was going to be the slow movement of an oboe concerto that he was writing for Harold Gomberg. Typical of Barber, he loved beautiful, heart-touching melodies. In fact, he is quoted of having said, "I give my most beautiful melodies to the oboe." A great example is in his Violin Concerto, where he wrote an incredibly beautiful oboe solo.

In the middle of writing the *Canzonetta* he was diagnosed with cancer and couldn't continue. He stopped writing. The manuscript of this one movement is in what is known as a short score. The accompaniment is basically written as a piano part, with arrows indicating the intended orchestration, and the oboe line. Charles Turner,[37] who had been a student of Barber's, completed writing the initial conceptualization.

The piece reminds me very much of Barber's *Adagio for Strings*, which is so famous, but the *Canzonetta* adds oboe. So I often jokingly say, "It's the 'Adagio for Strings,' with a maraschino cherry on top."

Sometimes when I have played it, I have nearly had to stop, because I am close to tears. An artist can't do that; get so drawn into your own expression. You have to be an observer. This did happen to me once. When I was playing at the funeral of a friend, I had to stop in the middle of the performance.

I saw this happen to Schwarzkopf once at a concert at Orchestra Hall in Chicago, where I was ushering. She was singing—in fact, it was an operetta. She was to sing this very, beautiful aria from the operetta. The orchestra played the opening, and then she was supposed to come in. But she was so moved that she stopped and said, "I can't. I can't. I can't." You can never allow yourself to be so overcome. You're the performer. The audience has paid money, so you must do it. No exceptions.

I enjoyed playing the Francis Poulenc Sonata for Oboe and Piano with you. I will keep that concert in my most precious memories forever.

Thank you. I appreciate that you feel that way.

I remember, the first time we played it you said, "Daniel, you must listen to me more." What is your perspective about this important work and about Poulenc's music?

As a young student in the 1950s, it was fashionable for academics and students to think that Poulenc was superficial, that his music was strictly on the surface, that it was not profound. At the time I thought so too. I was a child of those times. Later, I changed my mind. Poulenc reminded me of Truman Capote. Capote's public persona was casual and flippant. Appearing to take nothing seriously, he just cracked penetrating jokes. He was evasive; people didn't know what he was really thinking.

When Capote was still living, I did not have a high opinion of him. I thought he was superficial but when I saw the movie *Capote*, I realized that his superficiality was a mask. He hid his feelings behind the mask. He apparently felt so deeply that, if he really let his feelings show and let people know the depth of his sensitivity, he would be destroyed. It was too much for him. After seeing that film, I thought "What a fool I am. Why did I not see through it? Why did I not see the depth and profundity of this man?"

That's true of Poulenc as well. His compositions masked his true feelings. Many of us do that. You and I know people who live behind a mask. I must stop judging people. My father never judged.

---

37   Charles Turner (1921–2003), American composer, violinist and teacher, and one of the few of Barber's students.

And what about the Sonata in particular?

The Sonata was dedicated to Prokofiev, and much of it sounds like Prokofiev. Prokofiev and Poulenc were close friends. Poulenc may have kept his personal life private, because at that time, being gay was unacceptable. People who knew him, all of his friends in Paris knew him. I don't think Poulenc and Prokofiev were anything more than friends. It didn't matter, but his music had that quality of being concealed. He was dedicated. His craft was phenomenal. It is profound writing. The Dialogues of the Carmelites and Gloria are magnificent works that probe very deeply into the soul.

I remember you mentioned that the Sonata had some moments that echo Prokofiev's Romeo and Juliet.

Yes, the second movement is very fast, upbeat, as though he is trying to forget the death of a friend, and then, suddenly, a slow section that for me resembles the balcony scene in Prokofiev's Romeo and Juliet interrupts. It's an emotional, loving moment that reflects the depth of feeling, of the privacy of true friendship. In this same passage, it also sounds a bit like Gershwin. I can't document it, but I was told that Gershwin was rumored to have studied with Poulenc. In fact, I understand when Gershwin wrote American in Paris, Poulenc had been commissioned by Columbia Records to write A Frenchman in New York. He never wrote it. Those two pieces were supposed to be on the same album, but it never came to pass.

To me the whole Sonata is an elegy. In fact, the first movement is called, "Elegy." It is dedicated to the death and the loss of an intimate friend. You can hear it throughout the piece. The first movement begins with the oboe weeping alone. In the fast movement, he seems to be saying, "Forget about it; forget about it." Underneath, you can still hear the sadness.

Particularly in the last few bars of the piece.

Yes. I played that piece in concert commemorating the first anniversary of 9/11. The music brought everyone—including me—to tears. It was an emotional moment. I tried to remain objective to avoid being physically incapacitated by the expression that the piece had to convey to the listeners.

On only one occasion I was forced to halt my playing in mid-performance from the tears. It was at the funeral of a friend who had been murdered. Her husband asked me to play. There was an illustrious audience who were friends of her, including Henry Kissinger. It was a personal gathering of close friends.

I became too emotional because Alice had profoundly affected me. She was in her mid to late twenties. I was in my early thirties. She and her husband were good friends of mine. In fact, she and I had gone on vacation together to a cabin in Pennsylvania where we spent a week being very philosophical. During that week, we talked about everything, and our conversations opened my mind to a universe that I had never understood before.

Another French composer, Camille Saint-Saëns also wrote an important Sonata for Oboe, Op. 166, which he composed in 1921. How is this sonata different from Poulenc's work, and what are the most distinct aspects of this work?

My old recording of the Saint-Saëns from 1968 has recently been reissued. One of my students wrote the program notes for it. It is a very outgoing piece. Apparently there is very little known about the circumstances surrounding this piece. The first movement has the feeling of a Baroque siciliano. The oboe is ubiquitous in Baroque music, so Saint-Saëns wrote a French, modernistic piece that pays tribute to the French baroque, by way of the oboe sonority.

In the beginning of the second movement the oboe sounds almost like yodeling, reminiscent of the Swiss Alps, and then it plays a very pretty, pastoral theme that is typical for the oboe. He must not have known what to do with the last movement, so he wrote music that is better suited to violin. This movement is awkward to play, but very effective. Audiences love it. It is a great showpiece. You reminded me once not to forget when playing this piece that Saint-Saëns was also an organist. The chord structures and harmonic motion resemble the sonority of an organ.

Yes, Saint-Saëns was a child prodigy, equally skillful on both organ and piano. We talked briefly about Benjamin Britten's Six Metamorphoses after Ovid, Op. 49. What can you say about this particular work, which is for unaccompanied oboe?

The piece has six movements that are distinctive characters based on Ovid's Metamorphoses,[38] and are strongly programmatic in a way that is very descriptive of each character. In fact, every movement has a two-line narrative naming and describing the characters. I developed my own ideas about what each one was saying, and when in the music the actual metamorphosis takes place. These thoughts are personal. All oboists have their own ideas about the specific nature of this work. I love playing it, but doing all six on one concert is not necessarily the best idea, because it can be too much for the audience to take in at one time. I typically play four of them.

They do allow for some unusual programming. I did all six with my friend Renée Siebert, the distinguished flutist, in a trio that we had with a harpsichordist. Before I played, Renée read the accompanying two-line narrative to the audience. When she played, I did the readings. The audience loved it. Doing them alternately with flute and oboe is effective because the tone color shifts. The oboe tone is pungent. It is so distinctive that it can become overbearing so the listeners need some relief, but they are beautiful pieces.

One of the other important compositions Britten wrote for oboe is the *Phantasy Quartet*, Op. 2, which I also recorded when I was thirty-four years old. Although he was a prolific composer, he didn't begin numbering the opuses until they were concert pieces rather than pieces written for a particular occasion. He was a pacifist and devoted much time and

---

38 Ovid (aka Publius Ovidius Naso), Roman poet who lived between 43 BC and 17 or 18 AD.

attention when he was young to writing anti-war film music. This quartet is also about war.

It begins with a march marked *Alla marcia,* which has a metronome marking slower than a typical march. Britten's metronome marking is 96. A typical march is 120. It makes me think that Britten was specific in expressing hesitancy about going to war. At first, the march should lack the forward motion of a generic march. In fact, the tempo in my recording of the piece is too fast. I was recording with colleagues who were older and more experienced than myself and I didn't feel I had a right to tell them what my idea was. Mistake! After a brief cadenza, the mood shifts abruptly, it speeds into a much faster tempo than a typical march and is catapulted into the chaos of war.

Britten won the Cobbett Prize in 1932 for this piece. It was the first composition to bring him international recognition. It was also one of the first pieces that I recorded. That it is being reissued as a CD and once again available is an honor for me. This has happened through the kindness of Nicholas Fritsch, the son of the man who founded Lyrichord Discs, who had the idea of reissuing these performances.

In his own casual way, Nicholas's father, Peter Fritsch, whose son-in-law happened to be James Agee, was a very wise person. Peter once said something to me that stuck in my mind forever. He said, "I hate an idea whose time has come." In this regard I now often quote Ray Still to my own students: "If you think you know how to play the oboe, quit. Give it up. It's over." The beauty lies in the process, in the struggle. That is the joy of it.

As a genre, the oboe concerto form seems to have appealed much more to composers of the late twentieth century and now to composers of the twenty-first century than in the past. I have researched a bit and discovered a significant repertoire of contemporary oboe concertos. I think this may be because artists-in-residence at universities are writing music commissioned by orchestras and foundations. Do you keep current with new music, written recently or within the last twenty-five to fifty years? The conductor Esa-Pekka Salonen, for example, has composed an oboe concerto called Mimo II.

Well, first, I must wonder about your idea that more oboe concerti are written now than in the past. Some pieces survive, but many others do not. When I was performing concertos I enjoyed looking for works that were not well known. For example, Ludwig Auguste Lebrun,[39] a lesser-known contemporary of Beethoven, wrote a very good concerto that has largely been forgotten. Quite a few composers lived and worked in Vienna in Beethoven's generation. Their music was performed at the time, but a lot of it has not survived.

Concerti are usually written for a specific performer, a soloist, all the way from Friederich Rahm to Leon Goossens. Performers inspire composers. In earlier eras, money for new music came from the aristocracy. Now, it comes from foundations and the academe.

---

39 Ludwig Auguste Lebrun (1752–1790), German oboist and composer.

We can't predict which contemporary composers will be remembered in the future, which pieces will remain in the repertory. Vivaldi was popular in his time. So were Handel and many others. They traveled throughout Western Europe. Ironically, Bach never left Germany, but he became more important in history.

Shall we talk a little more about oboe repertoire? I know that one of your favorite chamber-music compositions that features the oboe is Mozart's Gran Partita.

Yes!

Will you share some insights about this magnificent work?

Well, my immediate reaction to that question is that Mozart wrote it unselfconsciously. He was not trying especially to write a great piece of music. He was just simply doing what came naturally to him. But the result was exactly that; a great piece of extraordinary writing. As a performer, I wish that I could always play as Mozart wrote, without any calculation or premeditation.

We wish to live our lives without premeditation, without calculation, don't we? Just to live. It's very difficult. We invariably worry about how we appear, or what others think, or what we think. Stop thinking. Just do it. I feel that the idea of "no thinking, just doing" prevails in the *Gran Partita.* It's magnificent; just a natural outpouring of talent and accomplishment.

Wouldn't it be wonderful to meet Mozart, to see what's inside his mind; to see if you could figure out what was inside that soul? Of course, in a sense, every time you play Mozart you are meeting him. You are discovering the interior of his soul. Maybe the outside, what he showed in public did not match the inside. I don't know. But as I play, I ask those questions.

It is an incredible piece; each note belongs, not one note is out of place. It has been a privilege to play that work. That's all I can say.

Perhaps meeting Mozart or anyone for that matter wouldn't help at all.

Exactly. If you met him, he might say that he is directly the opposite of what he expresses as a composer. He might even hide himself a little bit. My mind goes again to Truman Capote. He is not alone. I have met others who conceal themselves from scrutiny. I think sometimes we all do the same.

Arguably, Robert Schumann is one of the most expressive and intimate composers of all time. Luckily, he composed some wonderful works for oboe, for example the three Romances for Oboe and Piano, Op. 94. I know you love these pieces. Can you explain why?

I am not much of a scholar, but I have learned a lot from those who are. I am told that Schumann wrote these pieces because his wife Clara told him that he didn't know how to write well for oboe and needed practice. So he wrote these three pieces and gave them to her as a Christmas gift. I related this story to a student and he said to me, "So, Schumann proved he couldn't write for oboe. They don't belong on the oboe." Students are sometimes so wonderfully audacious! I wish sometimes that they could do this when they play!

Some of the works that Schumann wrote for the oboe are in A minor. The first and third of the three Romances are in A minor; the second is in A major. His Piano Concerto, which contains some important music for oboe, is in A minor. The "Romanza" movement of the Fourth Symphony is almost a concerto for oboe. That movement is written in A minor. He seemed to associate that pitch with the oboe. Someone told me he suffered from what we now call tinnitus, a perpetual sound in his ear that tormented him. It was an A.

It would not be surprising if Clara may have told him to practice writing for oboe because the Piano Concerto begins with a gorgeous theme for solo oboe. In the last movement a couple of passages given to the oboe are almost impossible to play, even on a modern instrument. And at that time, the oboe was not as agile. Do you remember the passage?

Yes, I do.

Those passages go to a high Eb. A high Eb on the oboe is not such a friendly note. Missing it is all too easy. We oboists have our tricks now, and I have learned to play that note accurately almost every time. But in those days, I can easily imagine that ninety percent of the oboe players who played that piece in concert did not get the note out. And so that may be what Clara was thinking when she said, "You don't know how to write for the oboe." It was that very specific, horrible high Eb.

You are correct about the Romances. They are three gorgeous pieces. The trouble with them is performance. I don't know that he meant them really to be performed together. They are so similar. They are mostly in the same tempo and they are all in three-part song form.

These pieces are not digitally difficult. They are all somewhat slow and musically challenging. Only one section, in the second movement, contrasts with dramatic intensity. But the rest of the set is just very, very beautiful.

The pieces have the same simplicity and profundity as Mozart or Schubert. I don't hear calculation in them. I hear Schumann falling deeper inside himself. At moments in these pieces, you can hear him getting depressed. You can hear a spiraling depression. Bloom, my teacher, said a wonderful thing about these pieces, that you shouldn't play them until you are at least forty-five years old and have been divorced twice.

They require a kind of experience, you know? I played them in my senior recital at the Chicago Musical College. But I didn't really perform them. You heard me play them at the Newport Music Festival. Do you remember? I think that was one of my better performances.

Well, I have heard you play live only a few times but I was completely mesmerized by your sound and your nuances, especially in the John Corigliano concerto.

There is a video of that performance.

Oh, it would be great to see it.

It is available on YouTube.

Bert, among your diverse activities as a musician is transcribing works for other instruments to the oboe. You transcribed a Schumann violin sonata for oboe, and also a movement from the soundtrack to The Mission. Can you tell me about these experiences? What were the challenges?

Ray Still encouraged me to do transcriptions; to take great, classical standards and adapt them for oboe. He was not much in favor of a lot of contemporary music. He thought most of it was nonsense. In fact, he described even the Vaughan Williams concerto as "noodle music, noodles noodling." He didn't give it the time of day. He preferred only a limited repertory. The period from Bach, Mozart to Brahms, completely captivated him-; maybe some Strauss and Mahler. Adapting a violin piece for oboe tells the listener that the work has sufficient universal merit to survive being played on another instrument. Playing a violin piece on an oboe can give it a whole new perspective. A great piece will survive the transition.

Schumann gave his publisher permission to include on the title page of the Romances, "for oboe or violin." The publisher added not only violin, but also clarinet. I understand that Schumann, enraged by this presumption, told the publisher that if he had wanted to write a clarinet piece, he would have written a clarinet piece. Which he did write later. Seems he didn't like the idea at the time of doing the Romances on a clarinet, but I have heard some wonderful clarinetists play them beautifully. Clarinetists can do things with it that we can't do on the oboe, certain nuances that are perfectly appropriate for the piece. The set was actually premiered on violin. It was not played publicly on oboe until fourteen years later. It's an incredibly difficult set for oboe; endurance again is a really big problem.

Every instrument can bring its own perspective. I have transcribed Schumann's *Adagio and Allegro,* a beautiful French horn piece, for oboe. Can you imagine playing a French horn piece on oboe? But it works. It is gorgeous. It has been played often on the cello. I understand that one of its most moving performances was of Rostropovich playing it at the Kennedy inauguration in 1961. That would be really wonderful to hear.

During the Baroque Era, pieces were played on any number of instruments interchangeably—flute, oboe, violin. Even Handel played oboe.

They played on any instrument that was available to them.

I think so. And they had to sell music. They were practical. Very few pieces are so idiomatic that they cannot be played on another instrument. Even Mozart transcribed his own Oboe Concerto for flute and the C-minor Wind Octet for strings.

We actually don't have the original manuscript for the Oboe Concerto; it was lost. But we do know that it was originally written for oboe, in the key of C major. We have no idea of what Mozart really wrote for the oboe part. Many players simply transpose the flute version, which is in D major, to C major for oboe. But certain sections of the flute part are not practical on oboe. In some of the octave passages, the oboe sounds like a squeaky wheel. So we oboists feel obliged—and justified—to alter the flute version, given our perspective. If I were sitting with Mozart as he composed, I would say, "Oh, please don't do that." I am comfortable saying silly things like that to a composer.

Corigliano's concerto works only on oboe. He made that choice deliberately. So there is no rule. Each player comes at this problem with his own perspective or sense of it. That's one of the wonderful things about art; and maybe about life. Later in his compositional output, Mozart became more instrument and performance specific.

One of the best examples of instrument transcription is, perhaps, the music of Johann Sebastian Bach, which has been transcribed into numerous and diverse combinations of instruments. The Goldberg Variations, for example, originally composed for a two-manual harpsichord, have been performed by a brass ensemble and they sound wonderful. Can you imagine? And I think one of the most frequently transcribed pieces of music is Ravel's Pavane pour une infante défunte. It sold many, many copies for different combinations of instruments, even during his lifetime, because he had to make money.

Even I recorded the Ravel.

Yes. So, if the music is good and the performer is good, it probably doesn't matter if you are playing oboe or ukulele.

Great music is great music. I like to say that you can view art from so many prisms. In music each instrument brings its own point of view and has its own prism through which to view the work. And all are legitimate. Every musician plays the Pavane differently. Does that mean that my playing of the same piece is superior to yours? Well, it could be, but we all have a right to co-exist.

Yes. Even the same piece of music on the same instrument can be completely different, depending upon the performer. I had this experience with some of the Alexander Scriabin preludes that I have been practicing. When I first heard them, I really didn't appreciate the Op. 11 set so much. Then after hearing Sofronitzky's recording,[40] I fell completely in love with them. I hardly recognized them as the same set. Since the middle of the twentieth century, the so-called historicist trend of performing has become more fashionable. We can count a long list of performers who play certain compositions only on the specific instruments for which they were originally written and they search in-depth for historic accuracy. What do you think about that?

The debate is about authenticity for me is a mistaken discussion. It is way too narrow. We will never know what a Baroque oboe really sounded like. We will never know what Bach's compositions really sounded like at the time of their conception, neither the tempi, nor the articulation or

---

40 Vladimir Sofronitzky (1901–1961), Russian pianist who married Alexander Scriabin's daughter Elena.

so many other aspects. He added articulation in only a few of his pieces. Articulation is another wonderful word. It is not only about whether you play legato or detaché. I have been to master classes by great jazz players who use the word articulation in its true sense. It is how you speak to give meaning, as you create the language of the piece. We have virtually no idea about the actual authenticity of the sound. In those days, even pitch was different. Authenticity? Really? I'm sorry, excuse me, but for me that's a little bit preposterous, unless you have a recording. And even then you are on thin ice.

When I play a piece that is centuries old, I go for the authenticity of what I imagine to be the composers intention and audience's response. If, listening to a particular piece I think that Bach's audience laughed, then I want my audience to laugh. If I think that Bach's audience cried, I hope my audience will cry. I tire of hearing listeners come away from Baroque concerts saying, "Oh, how interesting that was." At its best, music should not be interesting. It should be moving. It should be profound. Art should transform. It should change your life. It's not interesting. *Interesting* will kill classical music. Sorry. I don't mean to get excited.

Now, I would like to put you in a hard place and ask you a whimsical question. You must choose. It may be hard to say, but I want you to try to come up with an answer. I am sure you have been asked this question before. If you were to go to a desert island, and you could take only one piece of music with you to listen to, which piece would it be?

Not even just one composer, you mean one piece of music? Give me a break!

Okay Bert, let's say one composer.

One composer for me? I have thought about this—a lot. For me, it would have to be Mozart.

Mozart?

I have a feeling you're thinking Bach. Bach has characteristics that are incredibly wonderful—and Beethoven, and Schubert. Now we are back to the fun of Tomassini. But with Mozart, I think I told you once that, no matter how sad or melancholy he gets, he always has hope. Life is about hope. The only reason we want to live is because we hope that the next breath will make us better. I should avoid delving into politics, but...

Oh, please do.

The terrorists try to kill hope. If nothing else, what the United States represents in the world is hope, the hope of a better life, the hope of becoming more. They try to kill that sense of hope. People die trying to come to this country. No matter how misguided our politics can be at times; because this country remains a place of hope. For that reason, no matter what, I will always respect America. Because of their frustration, terrorists try to kill that hope. They will never succeed. Likewise dictators; they try to kill hope. Mozart embodies hope.

Absolutely. Let's talk about other major composers. Shall we start with Bach?

Bach enters the spirit through the mind. We know he was a numerologist. He plays that numerical game, so you become aware of the technique; nevertheless, Bach enters the spiritual mind. With Mozart, you never see the technique. All great composers have something. They have their own voice.

What about Beethoven?

For me Beethoven's seriousness is the key to the wonder of his music. Don't you want to be serious and proclaim that part of you—your spirit? Even when he is light-hearted, like in the Pastoral Symphony, he is seriously funny.

This statement may be dangerous, but Beethoven was, perhaps, the first composer to expand the emotional range to unexplored realms; that none before him had ever reached, not Haydn, not Mozart, not Bach.

Yes. I like your phrase, "unexplored realms," because it is so true. With Bach, I hear an emotional range, all the way from—one of my favorite pieces—the epic opening to the St. Matthew Passion, to some pieces that are guileless. You know, Bach wrote some light things, as did Mahler. But Beethoven took music to a place that was unforeseen—that we didn't know. He takes us into the unknown. Mozart, not so much unknown as unthought-of. Mozart puts a flashlight on his subjects.

Beethoven was, in my opinion, the first composer to speak directly to unknown emotions. That's why—and this perspective comes from non-musicians—he reaches people directly. My mother, for instance, loves Beethoven. She is completely crazy about Beethoven. Mozart, on the other hand, says nothing to her.

My father said, "Mozart all sounds the same."

It is fascinating, isn't it?

Exactly. Rock 'n' rollers love Beethoven. I think it's because of the internal energy of the music. You know, when I hear certain rock 'n' roll rhythms, it seems they are taken right out of Beethoven.

And Schubert?

Whew. Well, okay. So, Schubert—

I am making you think now.

Yes. Just yesterday I was listening to the Symphony in C Major. For me, Schubert is like that daisy we talked about in the Proust Questionnaire. Schubert, deceptively, creates the illusion of simplicity.

The Ninth, "Great C Major," Schubert's last symphony?

Yes. Oh! Schubert was able to express an incredible innocence. But that doesn't mean that his music doesn't have depth. Beneath that naïveté lies something very profound. He is like some intensely flavored food. He has a superb surface sound that also contains resonance and depth.

Schubert conveys less conflict than Beethoven, don't you agree? With Beethoven, conflict is ever present.

Oh, yes. In fact, that's a good description of the language of Beethoven's music: struggle.

Some old oboes acquired on various tours in Asia.

Roll-top desk found on West 73rd Street between Amsterdam and Columbus Avenues, Manhattan 1966. Dragged it down the street to my apartment. My cabinetmaker father restored it to perfection. It hides all of my reed secrets and sins!

Chapter 9. Oboeing

20 years of reeds from notable performances and recordings

Daniel Pereira: I know this question may put you in a hard place, but who are your favorite oboe players of the past or present?

Humbert Lucarelli: Oh no, you are not going to get me to make the Tommasini mistake. I don't have that much courage. Okay, I'll stick my neck out a little. In the early years of my career, my orientation was only toward American orchestral players. When I was studying the oboe, long-playing records were the story, and not many American oboe players did solo work. I heard American oboists mostly in recordings of orchestral performances. Obviously, I loved best my two teachers, Robert Bloom and Ray Still. But I also greatly admired Harold Gomberg[41] in the New York Philharmonic and Marc Lifschey[42] in the Cleveland Orchestra, John de Lancie in Philadelphia as well as others who came later, like John Mack.

We students used to play what I call the "distillation game." We tried to distill an artist's work into one word. Have you ever done this with pianists; describe them in just one word?

No, I have never made the attempt.

It's fun. For instance, Bloom was a poet. Ray Still was always exciting, took a lot of chances and deeply committed. Gomberg was a colorist. You must listen to those early Bernstein recordings of Mahler. You'll hear him playing. He pulls such exquisite colors from the oboe; an incredible rainbow of colors. Marc Lifschey's playing for me was liquid all the time. It flowed like honey.

---

41 Harold Gomberg (1916–1985), American oboist, principal of the New York Philharmonic from 1943–1977.

42 Mark Lifschey (1926–2000), American oboist, who held positions with San Francisco Symphony, National Symphony, Metropolitan Opera Orchestra and Cleveland Orchestra.

Another magnificent player was John de Lancie in Philadelphia. John de Lancie,[43] was very thoughtful and exquisitely musical. He was profoundly accomplished at the instrument and the music. I loved hearing him play.

Another great player was Alfred Genovese.[44] For many years, he was principal oboist for the Metropolitan Opera orchestra. His wife was a singer, and he was a lyrical, natural player. He seemed not at all studied. The music appeared to simply come out of him. Of course, as we all know, that's not the case with anyone. Natural talent takes years of work.

There are also European oboists who I didn't know very well, such as Lothar Koch[45] who played with the Berlin Philharmonic. His work was far from typical in an American sense, but he was undeniably musical—inspired and inspiring, expressive and profound. Whenever he played, he created magic. He moved the listener. The English oboist, Léon Goossens,[46] was also impressive. He inspired composers to write for him and helped create a repertoire that is still performed today. Other European oboe players from the past come to mind immediately, but there were many more like Andre Lardrot[47] or Omar Zoboli[48] and others.

It would be impossible to talk about proponents of the oboe without mentioning the ubiquitous and extraordinary Heinz Holliger who has contributed over fifty years to the instrument.

I loved all these players as individuals. Their authentic musicality always came through. Success comes because a player is believable, because he does what he does better than anyone else. Never try to be someone you are not.

Bert, could you talk more about your principal teachers, Robert Bloom and Ray Still?

Yes. As I said, Bloom was a poet. When he played, you felt he was speaking directly to you, in a very profound and personal way. And still—oh, I loved to compare Ray Still to Evil Knievel[49], the daredevil. Knievel used to fly on his motorcycle, made his living doing risky stunts. Ray Still was like that, because, when he played, he took chances. Hearing him play was thrilling, because he took the music to unimagined realms.

He said to me one time: "Making music is like performing in a circus—even if it is playing classical music. People want to hear you on the edge of making a mistake or doing too much. But you don't make a mistake. If you are good you can create the illusion of being on the edge, but you are really in control. You are still there, still present."

---

43 John de Lancie (1921–2002), American oboist, who was principal with the Philadelphia Orchestra for many years.

44 Alfred Genovese (1931–2011), born in Philadelphia, was principal of Boston Symphony and Metropolitan Opera.

45 Lothar Koch (1935–2003), German oboist, and one of the principals of the Berlin Philharmonic under Karajan's tenure.

46 Léon Goossens (1897–1988), British oboist.

47 Andre Lardrot, French oboist.

48 Omar Zoboli (b. 1953), Italian oboist.

49 Evil Knievel (1938–2007), American entertainer and international icon.

One year I played in the orchestra for the Ice Capades at Madison Square Garden. Every night the skaters ended the show, by locking arms and skating around in a circle. As they went around the rink, single skaters joining the line, one after the other. Completing this finale took about five or six minutes but, finally, the entire line was skating, sweeping in a circle on the ice. The last person to join had to skate very fast to catch up. Every night he almost missed—and almost fell—and the audience screamed, from fear and empathetic anticipation. But he didn't miss, and he didn't fall. You knew that he knew what he was doing. We musicians do the same thing. We make the audience think that we are at the edge; but we better not be if we want to get paid the next time!

What is your assessment of players currently working in orchestras or ensembles?

Come on! Oh, so many good players, and I may forget some—leave them out, by accident. I don't mean to, you know. In the end, I respect any musician who is out in the world playing. I respect any player who can earn a living and pay their rent playing the oboe. This is so hard to talk about.

Currently, America has some very special players. Richard Woodhams,[50] celebrated principal oboist of The Philadelphia Orchestra, an American oboist, brings a nuance and depth to every note he plays. Well-known American players are performing mostly with orchestras. I have to mention Liang Wang, who plays with the New York Philharmonic. He is an oboist of such astonishing ability that I can not imagine a piece he could not play. Eugene Izotov in Chicago, now in San Francisco is an elegant musician. Although no one has followed me yet primarily doing solo work, I hope that will happen. Alex Klein[51] formerly of The Chicago Symphony is also a good model for whom I have enormous respect. He has made a substantial discography and a major effort in this respect. Although Steve Taylor is not a member of a "major" orchestra, I cannot leave him out. He is oboist of the Lincoln Center Chamber Music Society and several other important chamber orchestras.

I have to tell you about a recent email I got from Jerry Kaplan, who is a great fan of the oboe. In fact, he taught me the most about how to make reeds. Jerry is the attorney who defended Ray Still when Ray was fired from the CSO and he also got my sister her three divorces, a great guy who knows a lot about oboe playing. The email reads, "Yesterday there was a two-hour program on PBS celebrating the liberal catholic popes. The orchestra was the, The Orchestra of St. Lukes. [sic] The oboe playing was glorious. I looked up the name of the principle oboe, Stephen Taylor…tell him that Jerry Kaplan, Ray Still's worst student, thinks that Stephen Taylor, is now the best oboe player playing in an American orchestra."

---

50   Richard Woodhams (b. 1949): current principal of the Philadelphia Orchestra.

51   Alex Klein (b. 1964): Brazilian oboist.

My knowledge of European and Asian players is very limited. But in Europe, I would have to name Albrecht Mayer[52] and Jonathan Kelly[53], who are both with the Berlin Philharmonic. Mayer is in the middle of developing a much-deserved career as a world-class soloist. Jonathan, who has more recently arrived at the Berlin Philharmonic, has made a great impact on me as a musician and artist of genuine substance. There are so many more. Gordon Hunt, who plays with the Philharmonia Orchestra in London, is an example of musicianship and accomplishment on the oboe at its highest level. There are also a couple others who I know well in Europe. Casey Hill, a former student of mine who has gone on to become a genuine artist and is Solo Oboist of the Orquesta Sinfónica de Galicia in Spain. Christian Wetzel, professor for oboe at the Academy for Music and Theatre in Leipzig, who is a genius teacher and a performer that always makes me want to listen.

There is also Washington Barella, who is also a former student of mine, who is a brilliant oboist and musician and has an extensive career in Europe as soloist and orchestral player, who is now teaching at Universität der Künste in Berlin.

These names are fresh in my mind at the moment. The ones that do not come immediately to mind all know who they are, and I know who they are. But I am leaving out so many great players. I hope they will forgive me.

I know when I go to sleep tonight they will all haunt me.

Can you talk more specifically about the particularities of different schools of oboe technique and oboe playing.

Ah! One of my favorite subjects! It's an enormous and controversial one, because it goes beyond oboe playing. First, I believe in my heart that until we oboists can put the subject of schools of playing aside, we can never really make the oboe a solo instrument. I understand that pianists assess a Russian school of playing, or an Italian school, or a French school. But in the end you don't condemn a pianist for having been trained in a particular school, nor do you to listen only to those who are in a specific school. We can be charmed, touched and educated by a wide variety of approaches.

National schools of playing are like country clubs. Musicians become part of a school because they think that a specific school credential will help them get a job. They wear the right tie, the right jacket, and they have an advantage. Not always true.

Every school has its own substance. But, in the end, rigidly adhering to a school of playing denies the individual. The individual cannot exist. This is anti-art. Art is a celebration of the individual, not a denial. As you can tell, I am passionate on this subject.

How can I listen to a German oboist like Lothar Koch or English oboist Gordon Hunt, who are so musical, and not appreciate them because they are in a different school from mine? Not possible. I don't respect such biased thinking. It's small minded, too narrow and petty.

---

52 Albrecht Mayer (b. 1965), German oboist.

53 Jonathan Kelly (b. 1969), English oboist.

Schools of playing, for me, are wonderful for their "costume interest." Wearing a costume, a Russian folk costume or lederhosen, for example, is charming. But deciding that it is the only way to dress is destructive. We all have national characteristics. We like to say that the Germans are intellectual, deep and profound, the French are suave and charming, and the Italians, open and loving. Those are clichés. For sure, clichés carry some truth; they exist for that kernel of truth. But it's not overbearing or substantive. We must look for individual substance, especially today when the world is so interconnected. This is important. We must recognize and celebrate the authenticity of individuality. The school doesn't matter.

But still there are different schools of oboe playing. Can you give me some examples of diametrically opposed tendencies, in both technique and approach to musical expression?

Now you are pushing! Some schools of playing and styles of playing have developed an original technique. Such techniques serve the aesthetic of both the individual and the environment. For instance, I know one oboe player in particular whose public persona is very conservative. His playing is the same. He has developed a style of playing and a technique that serves his personality. No one does it as well as he. It is beautiful to hear him play. Only fools don't respect that.

Other players wear their emotions on their sleeves; their playing is overtly expressive. They take chances; engage in daring acrobatics with the music. Their technique is built on the concept of extreme flexibility. One style is no better than the other. I say only that the style and the manner of playing serves the aesthetic of the individual and the environment in which it exists. It is possible that an oboist playing in an orchestra tends to be a more disciplined performer that fits in than someone whose career is as a soloist or chamber musician.

Within every environment can be found brilliant artists who develop their own style and their own technique. They attract acolytes who love, admire and emulate their playing; who become fans, in a manner of speaking. The disciples more often copy more the external than the substance; a regrettable situation.

In the United States, many oboists followed Marcel Tabuteau,[54] a magnificent player. None I know who studied with Tabuteau played like Tabuteau. In fact, the players who studied with him are so distinct and different from one another. So, what did he do for them? He released an internal creativity in each player and a reflection of their own artistry. Tabuteau developed a unique style of playing and expression that worked for him. At that time, no one else played as he did. He developed his own personality his own voice. He imitated no one. Great players create their own school by making their own rules. You create your own reality.

---

54 Marcel Tabuteau (1887–1966), French oboist, considered the founder of the American school of oboe playing.

John Mack,[55] who was a devoted student of Tabuteau, and I played the oboe very differently. We had differing aesthetic sensibilities and differing technical approaches to mastering the instrument a clear reflection of his aesthetic sense. We were good friends. One time, when Mack and I were halfway through a bottle of Scotch and joking around, I got very serious. And said, "John, I hope you don't mind. I don't play like you. And I hope that's okay for you."

He said such a beautiful thing; it brought tears to my eyes. He said to me, "You know, Bert, every time you play, I believe you." Well, that touched me very deeply because he was sometimes considered unyielding in music making and in playing the oboe. He showed me flexibility and a capacity to feel freedom. To say something like that was very, very moving to me.

That was a truly candid—and personal—moment for both of you.

That's artistry. He accepted me on a level that I could only dream of.

So, we both forgot schools of playing. People wear different clothes, different styles, and the French have their *haute couture*.[56] Visit the Metropolitan Museum's costume collection. Speaking of museums, you remember we spoke of the Barnes Collection in Philadelphia and its diverse collection of artists living within a span of about fifty years. They all have their own style and personality.

How could I forget such an experience?

That collection is only fifty years of art history, mostly in France. The distinction between painters in that museum is incredibly moving. They didn't all paint the same, despite their proximity in time and place. Monet, Manet, Toulouse-Lautrec and Picasso. They were unique and authentic. So, about this "schools-of-playing" business. These artists needed no country club membership. A club is unnecessary for a true artist. I am sure that you have heard enough. I'll get off my soapbox.

I could listen to you for my entire life and not hear enough. I need only a cup of coffee and some food.

And some cheese and bread.

Well, and let's not forget the wine. From the very beginning, you mention your sound. Can we talk about your oboe sound, which is so uniquely recognizable? Many elements can affect the oboe's tone quality: The reed, the instrument's design, the acoustic and the breath. Your sound is well known by many. How did you develop your tone and what elements are crucial to acquiring a beautiful sound on the oboe?

Well, it's not technical. It's not external. It's not in the reed; it's not in the oboe. You have it in your ear. I mean, forgive me, I have to ask you—you are a pianist. I have often told you that your sound is special. Was it this way for you from the beginning?

55 John Mack (1927–2006), American oboist.

56 Haute couture: the designing and making of high-quality fashionable clothes by leading fashion houses.

Yes, it was in many ways. I had to learn to control it, of course. It matured along with the development of my ear's sensibility. So the more sophisticated that the ear becomes, the more sophisticated and nuanced the sound will be.

So it was for me with the oboe. The technique I learned supported the sound conception that I already had in my ears. It wasn't the other way around. After I left Chicago and moved to New York I met with a young friend who had played with me in the All-State Orchestra, when we were in high school. She invited me to dinner one night and while we were having dinner she played a pirated recording of the Sibelius Second Symphony, with its big oboe solo in the second movement. And I said, "That is me!" After more than fifteen years of studying and playing professionally, I was still able to recognize my sound. It had not changed so much since high school. But I learned, as you said, to control it better, and use it with more sophistication. Studying with and listening to great musicians on every instrument is critical.

Studying with Bloom was fortuitous, because he perceived so much about working with sound. He understood what he heard. I don't mean to diminish Ray Still's influence. Still was more analytical. But Bloom could see when something completely eluded me, when I couldn't get the sound and do what I wanted. That possibility always looms on the piano as well. You put your hand in a position that impedes your sound and the result can be catastrophic.

Very true, Bert. Then let me ask you, is it a matter of training the ear and the body?

Yes. If you are teaching, you must be sensitive to that connection. You must recognize, for instance, that a student whose embouchure is distorted will never create the sound with the flexibility they desire. I told a student recently, "Your embouchure is not the problem, it is a symptom of the problem." A headache is a symptom. Tylenol or Aspirin will mask the symptom, but to fix it, you must go to the root of the problem. It could be lack of sleep, poor eating habits, stress or even some psychological problem.

Treating the symptom diminishes the aggravation, allowing the mind to relax and the body to heal. It is a little bit like meditation. Good doctors have told me that treating an illness means getting out of the way and letting the body heal itself; a little bit like Alexander Technique. This is true for playing an instrument. You must get out of the way, listen carefully. Trust your heart and your ear.

In connection with the sound, what are the secrets, if any at all, to making an excellent reed?

The reed doesn't make the sound. You make the sound. The reed is a facilitator, just as the oboe—the instrument—is a facilitator. As a pianist, you know yourself. I have heard pianists play on many different instruments, but they always somehow find a way to sound like themselves. It could be a junk instrument or a great instrument. They still find a way.

They do anything they have to do. You find a way for your own identity to come through in the sound. You can do that with a piano, and I can do that with a reed or with the oboe. You are correct, that some reeds invite me to play better, just as some pianos invite you to play better. In fact, they challenge us to play better than we think we can.

Well, when I play on a very good piano my fantasy and my imagination, in terms of the sound, rapidly expand.

In other words, hearing yourself sounding beautiful inspires you. You are propelled further, and you relax, to reach places where you might otherwise never dream of going. Don't you think? Good instruments and good halls inspire you.

I ask you about the reed, because so often I have heard oboe players say, "I played poorly, because my reed was in bad condition." What would you tell these players?

Yes. Well, it is true. Some players say that playing on good reeds is easy; you must learn to play on the bad ones. As Bloom told me once, "If you don't have the reed you like, learn to love the reed you have." Of course, I fell on the floor laughing, because that is again like everything in life. It is like relationships. Not every relationship is magic all the time; but you learn to love it, because it is important to you.

The Brazilian solo oboist Alex Klein said to me, "Bert, you amaze me. Every time we play a concert together, you have a good reed." But that's not the case. The point is that, no matter what the reed is, at every concert, I must play well. As Ray Still once said, "The audience pays money, and you must dance." It's funny, makes me think again, "We Can't Always Play Waltzes."

Let me tell you a little bit about reeds. Oboe players are obsessed with getting the right one and audiences are fascinated with the subject. Partly because most professional oboists physically make their own reeds; it's an unusual part of our craft of playing the instrument. There is a mystique and bit of magic about the process. In some regard we are making our own instrument. Like a singer, building their own voice.

So, Bert, what is a good reed?

What we call a good reed is simply a reed that allows us to make the sound we want. It does not make the sound. I keep saying, "It is a facilitator." In a way, like the instrument. The proof of that pudding is that I can give the same oboe and reed to ten different accomplished oboists and it will sound like ten different oboists. Conversely, I can give ten different oboes and reeds to one oboist and it will sound like one oboist. We make the oboe and reed do what we want and I repeat, "What we call a good reed is simply a reed [or oboe] that allows us to make the sound we want." How hard do we have to work to make it happen? Or, does it invite us to do what we want. That is what we call a good reed or a good oboe.

What is the reed made of?

The reed is made of a specific species of bamboo, or cane called "arundo donax." When I was a student in the mid-1950s, the best cane came from the south of France in what is the region of Fréjus north of the Rivera. Today, the choice has widened. There is good cane from China, Argentina, Spain, almost everywhere. The moon is next! The cane for making reeds is very much like wine grapes. Half mile down the road will produce a cane that has a very different inclination. Some can be softer, harder or have qualities that feel completely different. So we are on a constant search for just the right cane. The cane that will allow us to make the reed that will allow us to make the sound we want.

Then we have to process it with tools that take it only to within 0.60 mm near the bark with a machine called a gouger and then shape it into a carefully measured width and contour. There is a great deal of controversy among players as to what the exact optimum measurements are. Of course all of these measurements rely on just what you want to sound like and how you want to play. Obviously, a reed that works for me may be garbage for you.

After that you take the shaped and gouged piece of cane and tie it on to a tube or staple that fits into the top of the oboe. There is even controversy about what is the best tube to use. This tying process produces what is called a blank. Again, there is even controversy about how to tie the reeds. It is my personal opinion the process of making a good blank is more important than we like to admit. It is of course the foundation on which you build the reed. The simplest variation in the blank will affect everything about the scraping of the reed, like tying over the top of the tube.

You talk about scraping a reed. I've seen oboe players whittling on a reed with a knife. What is that about?

And, oh yes, the scraping. There are so many ideas and attitudes about how to scrape a reed that it can take a lifetime to come to it. John Mack used to say, "Scraping a reed a day keeps the shrink away. You have to make a barrel of bad reeds before you can make a good one." The process is a bit like Zen. Many players never really come to terms with this process. I can tell you I was not comfortable with it until I reached the age of forty-two, after playing and making reeds for almost thirty years. The variety of scraping techniques and styles is endless.

I don't want to get into the details here, but I can tell you that oboists talk about it all the time. The first thing one player asks the other is, "Where do you get your cane!" Next is, "How long do you tie the blank? Now I know why you're a good player or a bad player!" What silly nonsense.

If you lose your sense of humor about it you're in big trouble. I love making reeds because it puts me in very close touch with how I want to sound and play.

The oboe, Bert, seems to sing in your hands, just like an opera singer. Which singers from the past or present have most strongly influenced your music making and your conception of the nuances of the line?

I would say for sure Maria Callas,[57] Renata Tebaldi[58], Sutherland, Schwarzkopf, and Birgit Nilsson.[59] The list goes on and on. Again it is like asking me about oboe players. I love all of them for what they can do. I have stolen from all of them. They are so incredible, because they are able to do so much with the line and the intervals and the music. When you watch the score as they sing, every sixteenth note, every eighth note, every nuance that the composer wrote on the page, translates into sound. And yet it is all done with a personal quality as well. How they do that is a living lesson to me. So they are all very important.

Of course, there were Elizabeth Schwarzkopf, Christa Ludwig[60] and Teresa Stich-Randall.[61] Oh my God, so many great singers! Joan Sutherland, for me, was really very powerful, very different from Callas, because she reached into the soul of the music through supreme craftsmanship. Callas seemed to do it with a powerful, artistic internal mystical commitment. There were some male singers as well: Dietrich Fischer-Dieskau,[62] Eberhard Wächter[63] and Fritz Wunderlich,[64] all amazing singers.

We instrumentalists try to do what singers do. What enables a singer to transmit universal expressive qualities so well? If the interval weeps, you can hear the singer weep. And when the singer laughs, the whole line laughs. Do you recall Natalie Dessay's *Glitter and Be Gay*? Her performance is incomparable. It completely blows me away.

I am not quite sure why the interval seems to be the natural province of the voice. We could talk about how the intervals work, and stretching an interval of a fifth is different from an octave, if only because of a sheer difference in distance, especially when you are in the voice, because of the physical connection between the air and the vocal cords. I don't know how much truth is in it. You know? Forgive me for not knowing, but I think it is a good question to ask.

You know the craft is such an important part of the game. When I think of piano craft I think of Lang Lang. He is truly incredible. I know some people are not enamored of his playing, But, you have to respect it. It seems to me when he goes "off," the craft is so brilliant it seems to outshine what he is trying to say. I don't think it is intentional except once in a while you hear him say, "Watch this." That's okay, I can allow him that.

You know, now that he is getting older, I feel he is relying less on his craft and enjoying his desire to speak about the music. After all there are other

---

57 Maria Callas (1923–1977), American soprano of Greek descent.

58 Renata Tebaldi (1922–2004), Italian soprano.

59 Birgit Nilsson (1918–2005), Swedish dramatic soprano.

60 Christa Ludwig (b. 1928), German mezzo-soprano.

61 Teresa Stich-Randall (1927–2007), American soprano.

62 Dietrich Fischer-Dieskau (1925–2012), German baritone and conductor.

63 Eberhard Wächter (1929–1992), Austrian baritone.

64 Fritz Wunderlich (1930–1966), German tenor who tragically died in an accident.

players now who can play even faster, louder, with as much craft if not even more. I have always felt that you can't just bank on craft. Someone will come along who can play faster and cleaner, but no one can ever play with your persona and vision. The craft will get you in the door, but in the end you have to do something with it.

I will never forget Raya Garbisova who I spoke of before. We both taught at Hartt on Mondays and Tuesdays so we had dinner just about every week. One night she said to me, "It's a funny thing my fast movements are getting slower because as I get older there are more musical ideas that come in, and the slow movements are getting faster because I don't need so much time to say what I want to say. Everything is now coming out the same tempo!"

I get a feeling Lang Lang is getting to be the same except when he wants to be annoyingly (to some listeners) silly. I know the feeling. Please, let's not be mean, let's just laugh with him.

May we talk about oboe manufacturers? What oboe do you play, and what are the distinguishing characteristics of the various oboe brands; their sonorous qualities, construction materials and key work?

For many years, I have played a French oboe, the Lorée. It is a popular instrument with American oboists. François Lorée designed it with the guidance of Marcel Tabuteau, who I explained earlier was the leader of what became known as the American school of playing. Tabuteau's advice was crucial in the creation of the instrument's sonority. Its timbre is extraordinary. It has the possibility of a very special tone; the blend of overtones and the depth are exceptional.

Some other oboe makers I would rank as world-class are Marigaux in France, Mönnig in Germany and Howarth in England. Läubin and Covey are excellent American makers. Most recently Fox in the United States has developed a very special instrument they call the Soyen. Another French maker, the Rigoutat, is very popular in Europe. The great Heinz Holliger[65] loves to play the Rigoutat. The two principal players in the Berlin Philharmonic, Albrecht Mayer and Jonathan Kelly, ironically prefer different brands of oboes. Albert plays a Mönnig and Jonathan a Marigaux. In recent years, Howarth has become popular in the United States. There are others. They all have distinctive sonorous possibilities. I have a student, Heather Baxter, who recently got the principal job in Omaha, Nebraska playing a Yamaha. It's a perfect instrument for her. I would never force a student to play a particular brand of oboe.

These are exciting times for oboists because a variety of makers are coming up with wonderful new ideas for improving the design of the instrument. If I were performing today, I would have to examine all the options.

Many of the instrument makers I have mentioned have worked very diligently to resolve some of the problems of playing the instrument: intonation, color, flexibility and at the same time establishing their own

---

65   Heinz Holliger (b. 1939), Swiss oboist, composer and conductor.

personality. It is not that I want everything to be easy but, when it is less complicated, one can be free to be more expressive. You don't have to worry so much about accommodating the instrument. You are inspired and challenged by the instrument!

The Howarth is a fine example of an instrument that has improved enormously, in part because Lorée has been very generous to them and given Howarth the reamers, the tool that shapes the inside of the bore of the instrument.[66] The Mönnig instruments are a German brand that look for a deeper, maybe darker and stable tone than the others and pays particular attention to intonation. The French instruments facilitate more flexibility. But the choice really rests on what you are accustomed to; what you like, what you feel comfortable with. Isn't it the same with your choice of pianos?

Yes. I am inclined toward Steinway & Sons, some Yamahas and Bösendorfer. Fazioli is also becoming very popular, but it is quite expensive. Fazioli makes only about 120 instruments each year, whereas Steinway builds about 3,000.

So it is with oboes. The American oboe maker Läubin limits production to have quality control. Lorée builds many instruments each year. Its manufacturing facility is quite large. Quality control is a challenge with mass production but Lorée is dedicated to managing it very successfully. I have a special place in my heart for the Lorée family, but experimenting with other instruments is an important responsibility.

When you performed on tour, did you take several instruments with you, different brands?

My first oboe was a Rigoutat, purchased with money from the insurance company's settlement after my legs were shattered. I bought a used Rigoutat for $500. It was all I could afford. I also played the Läubin for a while, during my time with Ray Still. After 1961, when I studied with Bloom, I switched to Lorée and have stayed with it for the rest of my playing career.

I own only two Lorées. There is an old Lorée which you hear on most of my recordings. I still have that instrument. It is special and I still play it. There is also a new one that's about three years old. They both invite an extraordinary tone. Lorée gave me a plastic top joint, just the top, because wooden top joints[67] tend to crack if the temperature and humidity are not right. I always keep my good plastic top joint on hand. That's all I have— just the two instruments. Some players have as many as twelve instruments. That would be too confusing for me. I prefer to stay with one instrument. Bloom used to say, "Your instrument becomes like your best friend. You know what to expect of it."

---

66   The reamer is a tool that controls the internal contour of the board, which is the inside of the instrument and affects all aspects of the sound, tone and pitch.

67   Wooden joints are one of the three sections that make up a conventional oboe, which are top, bottom and bell.

Chapter 10. Career

Athens Greece in front of Parthenon on way to tour
Australia, 1973 Photo Credit Susan Muhlhauser

Daniel Pereira: *You have often been praised as a true oboe virtuoso. What does the word "virtuoso" mean to you?*

Humbert Lucarelli: To most people, I think it means that you can play a lot of notes very fast. In order to get the review[68] labeling me a virtuoso, I did exactly that: playing a lot of notes very fast. If you are going to be in the game, you have to play by the rules. You go out, and you do it. So, I learned to play a couple show pieces with incredible facility and speed, even if my heart was not in it.

Playing fast notes is measurable. I know how fast your notes are. I can put a metronome on them. I know how clean they are, by carefully listening to them. These are not subjective judgments; they are factual, objective notions, like the speed of a horse race or how many home runs you hit. More important for me is whether you can move the audience and whether you go into their heart. This is a subjective judgment and it is for me more difficult to accomplish; but you must trust your instinct. Bloom said to me that he trusted his own instincts on this subject. One could teach for a lifetime on this phenomenon.

So for me, a virtuoso is a musician who can speak, who can move the listener. A virtuoso has his own personality, his own character and his own quality.

---

68   The review praising Mr. Lucarelli as the leading American oboe recitalist appeared on the *New York Times* and was written by Allan Hughes.

He can take a work of art and bring it to life. In this sense, I always admired actors such as Alec Guinness or Meryl Streep. I wanted to be the Guinness or Meryl Streep of oboe players because of the wide array of characters and styles they are able to emote. When I played baroque music, I became a baroque player. When I performed twentieth-century music, I became a twentieth-century player. I tried to make myself always the best at any style I was playing. There is no best, of course. I tried to find the courage to bring my own best to every performance. That is a virtuoso.

You have been named America's leading oboe recitalist. You built your career mainly on solo and ensemble performances, in contrast to many oboe players in America who hold orchestra positions. Why did you embrace that path?

That's a specific field that I fell into pretty much by accident. Many orchestral players, whom I admire, deserve equal recognition.

I took the path of doing recitals because, when I came to New York, I couldn't find playing jobs. No one knew me. So I decided to do a recital, at what was then known as Carnegie Recital Hall, now Weil Recital Hall, to introduce myself to New York audiences. I applied for a grant from the Rockefeller Foundation and, after an audition the Foundation granted me the funds for a recital. I naively sent invitations to contractors who put orchestras together. Of course, none of the contractors attended, but Howard Klein from the *New York Times* did. Afterward he wrote a review, saying, "Bert Lucarelli is a wonderful oboe player and could play at any major orchestra in the country, but the oboe is not a solo instrument." Well, that was a problem for me, because don't ever tell me no. Never, never, never tell me it can't be done. Mr Klein came to my second recital three years later and declared it an ideal recital. Ha! I won him over. He and I later became friends. I became a soloist because of him.

So I started to study. I had to ask some questions. What is a recital? What is a recitalist? How can the oboe be a successful solo recital instrument? Some European oboists were successful recitalists. Not many American oboists at the time had even made recordings. My teacher, Robert Bloom, recorded. Mitch Miller, who was more well known as a record producer and conductor than as an oboist, had also done several solo recordings, as had a couple of other Americans, like Harold Gomberg and Harry Schulman. No one like Lothar Koch or Pierre Pierlot[69] or Leon Goossen had done multiple solo recordings. So I thought, "Hey, maybe an American should be represented." Just from total naïveté. Most of these records by celebrated oboists of the time were originally on LP and some are now available on CD and iTunes were funded by companies who sere subsidized by their governments.

It was about this time that I was playing as a "ringer" with what was then known as the Scranton Philharmonic, later to be the Northeastern Pennsylvania Philharmonic. A ringer is what is known as someone who is brought in to fill a position for which there is no local counterpart. The conductor of the Scranton Philharmonic was Beatrice Brown, one of the

---

69   Pierre Pierlot (1921–2007), French oboist.

first women conductors of a symphony orchestra in the United States. She was at Tanglewood studying with Serge Koussevitzky at the same time as Leonard Bernstein and Seiji Ozawa. After a couple of concerts she asked me to play a concerto with the orchestra. Because she was a champion of modern music, she chose the Oboe Concerto of Bohuslav Martinu. It was the first concerto I ever played with orchestra. She had courage.

It was there in Scranton at the home of the president of the orchestra Sondra Myers that I met the Reverend Norman Stanton, who had recently moved to New York City where he had become the Associate Pastor of The Madison Avenue Presbyterian Church. In these early days in New York I invented concerts, played anywhere for little or no money in the hope that someone would hear me. With some close friends we started a chamber music group that, with more than a little bit of grandiosity called ourselves The New York Bach Soloists patterned after the Bach Aria Group, but with more of an instrumental emphasis on repertory. The flutist was Bonnie Lichter who is one of the most honest and passionately dedicated musicians I have ever known and to this day remains one of my closest friends and also Gerald Rack a harpsichordist of incredible intensity.

The Reverend Norman Stanton gave us the space to perform at The Madison Avenue Presbyterian Church. Norman remains to this day one of the angels in my life.

So, I began my journey to become an oboe soloist. Thinking that imitating singers would be a good idea, I went to voice recitals. It was the "Golden Age" of vocal recitals in New York: Elisabeth Schwarzkopf, Dietrich Fischer-Dieskau, Christa Ludwig and Teresa Stratas were just a few. I even remember hearing Peter Pears with Benjamin Britten accompanying him on the piano in Schubert's *Winterreisse*. There were so many more. I studied their skill at communicating with the audience—walking onstage, where they stood, their bows—all of the elements necessary for building a successful recital persona.

I also studied acting, sculpting and painting in order to better understand communication. These disciplines put me in clear contact with the act of being creative. I knew I would find my persona only in realms other than music, because I had already studied with two of the most brilliant oboe teachers in the world. For this enterprise, I had to go elsewhere. So, I found my performance persona by studying other disciplines. It worked for me. As a young performer, I had developed an awkward, outgoing and exuberant personality, that many people found charming, which had to change as I matured. I had to find a way to go more inside where the real stuff is.

You have played in numerous orchestras and opera productions. Can you think of a piece or composer that you have not yet encountered, but would like to learn and play?

In the entire repertoire, orchestral, solo, everything, you mean?

Yes, something that you have never played, but wish that you had.

Well, I have never played Bruckner, and some pieces of Strauss, some of the operas. I love Die Frau ohne Schatten. I love Strauss. I heard that he once said that he believed himself to be a superficial composer. Interesting, how we judge ourselves. He also said, "I am like some wallpaper." That comment gives me a surrealistic vision of wallpaper that you sink into and disappear.

You have surely played every major piece in the repertoire.

Yes, I have played a lot. It is hard to say.

Have you played much twentieth-century music, let's say, the first composers to depart radically from tradition, Schönberg and the Second Viennese School?

My favorite experience in that style was playing Schönberg's Woodwind Quintet, which I think was his second twelve-tone piece, op. 26. It was fascinating, because I played it as if it were Romantic. I couldn't play any intervals unemotionally.

Oh, that is an unfair statement; that twelve-tone music's intervals are unemotional. Anyway, playing that piece was wonderful. It is a lengthy piece, maybe forty minutes. We learned it as a chamber piece, without conductor. Some performances have been conducted. Stravinsky's assistant Robert Craft, whom I mentioned earlier, conducted one great recorded performance with the Westwood Wind Quintet. Craft was a wonderful man and musician. He conducted this recording of the Schönberg Quintet because it was so complex, and he loved complexity.

But, you know, no matter how complex the music is, we just had to work on it. We spent a lot of time learning that piece. But, in the end, I still felt very romantic about it. I mentioned earlier *Die Frau ohne Schatten*. There are in *Die Frau ohne Schatten* sounds of twelve-tone music. It goes right to the edge. And yet, you could probably analyze it tonally. It is ridiculous, where tonality goes. It becomes a piece of over-ripe fruit. You can't hold it. It squishes in your hand.

What did you play with the Chicago Symphony Orchestra?

I played with the Chicago Symphony three times. One of my most unforgettable memories was playing in Berlioz's Symphonie fantastique at the Ravinia Festival. In the opening of the third movement, the English horn and an offstage oboe engage in a dialogue. So, I was directed to play the oboe, outdoors of course, in the bushes. And so I played my solo in the heart of nature. I will never forget that feeling.

I also remember playing Wagner under Fritz Reiner.[70] I had a tiny little solo. Reiner realized that I was new, so he gave me a cue that almost knocked me off my chair. With his finger, he said, "Go!" and pointed at me. Because his gesture was so forceful, I played too loud. My teacher Ray Still, who was sitting next to me, said, "Cool it. Just relax." But I was reacting to the intensity of Reiner's beat. And I think Reiner actually smiled. He had a funny way of smiling. His lips never went up; his eyes just twinkled.

---

[70] Fritz Reiner (1888–1963). Hungarian conductor.

You played at pianist Arthur Rubinstein's eightieth birthday celebration concert. Could you share some memories about that event?

It was a week-long celebration. We played three concerts, on Monday, Wednesday and Friday. Monday night was four Mozart concertos; Wednesday night, three Beethoven, ending with the "Emperor"; and Friday night, the two Brahms concertos. Rubinstein had the demeanor of a nineteen-year-old boy. It was unbelievable. He had so much energy. He danced around, getting up from the piano, sitting back down, playing, playing; he even played a flute part on the piano. He never stopped moving. He was so excited. Seeing him—at his age—with such energy and love for his art was such an inspiration.

Of course, more amazing was the rehearsal schedule. Before Monday night's concert, we rehearsed the Mozart with him that morning and, on Monday afternoon, we rehearsed Beethoven. So, we had rehearsals in the morning and afternoon, seven concertos and then a four-concerto concert that night. Truly, a pianist half his age could not match such stamina—and just to keep it all in his memory! Who has such facility and such ability with the mind? He was something else. He loved living and loved what he was doing—and could do it.

Where did these concerts take place?

Carnegie Hall, in New York.

And you played first oboe?

No, I was playing second. It was early in my career. I did a lot of second oboe playing in those days.

Do you remember the first chair oboist, sitting next to you?

Yes, it was Leonard Arner.[71] At the time he was New York's leading freelance oboe player. He had competed one-on-one with Ray Still for the Chicago Symphony's principal oboe position. When Still was chosen, Arner's career detoured into a very successful free-lance career in New York City. I played second oboe to him often in many important venues. He was a good colleague to me but he showed some occasional slight bitterness. It was the style in those days. Maybe it is now, too, with some instrumentalists. I don't want bitterness in my life. Who needs it? It gets in the way.

A frequent topic of conversation about chamber music and orchestral playing is the question of playing together. Should chamber and orchestral musicians invariably align together musically or is a little dislocation from time to time permissible? Is not falling quite on the beat at the same time, every time still within the realm of optimal musical expression?

I would say, as I understand your question, that a musician who plays slightly off needs to do so with intent. It is no accident. You allow it to happen. Great players do nothing arbitrarily. They allow for the moment, for creativity and

---

71 Leonard Arner (1924–2011), American oboist, founder and director of the Amadeus Ensemble.

for spontaneity. On the other hand, we must draw a line—the line that Ray Still implied, that we walk on a high wire, on the edge. Certainly, I am not always right. I try to be. And what is right, anyway? A Lexus automobile commercial tells the viewer: "We are in pursuit of perfection." It is a clever line, but we can't only be obsessed with perfection. The pursuit of perfection alone destroys creativity. A friend, Daniel Orr who is a celebrated chef, once said to me that the best recipes come from mistakes.

In chamber music and especially in orchestral music, the player must listen to all the music surrounding him, even more than to himself, because he must be aware of the whole more than only his own part. Great actors actively listen to one another as they work together. And maybe that's life. You've got to listen to everyone in the room. Otherwise, you are just alone. I'm so disappointed in myself when I don't listen to my friends.

Going back to Arthur Bloom who was the clarinetist in Lark Woodwind Quintet; we started the quintet about three years before the Corigliano Concerto commission, and I think this group was one of the most important influences on my musical life. It would be impossible to overstate how much I learned from my colleagues. The one thing they never seemed to be able to teach me was how not to be late for a rehearsal. It was a stupid insult to them on my part for which I have never forgiven myself.

It is fair to say one our most important efforts was a recording of works by Carl Nielsen for woodwinds that included the famous Quintet. I'm proud to say that the Quintet recording seemed to be a "benchmark" recording of that piece for several years.

During the entire history of the Lark Quintet the only personnel changes we had were in bassoon and horn. We could discuss for hours how the change of one person in a chamber music group affects the whole tone and musical attitude of a group.

Yet we loved playing with our first bassoonist Alan Brown, who's on the Nielsen recording, and who left to teach at the university in Puerto Rico. When Lenny Hindell joined the group, he brought a different perspective to everything we played. What I loved the most about Lenny's playing is that he made the bassoon sound like a beautiful viola. There was a warmth, gentleness and fluidity to his playing that reminded me of Marc Lifschey or Raphel Hillyer, the former violist of the Juilliard String Quartet, with whom I toured for three years in a trio. This discussion reminds me of an ad for a women's cologne I saw in the window of a drug store. The ad reminded me of Lenny's playing and what I wanted to emulate. It said, "Its strength is in its gentleness." That describes Lenny to perfection.

Our initial horn player was Bill Brown, who you can also hear on the recently re-released version of the Nielsen on Lyrichord Discs. Bill was a magnificent player. After Bill left, Jerry Warsaw replaced him, for only about a year, and if I remember correctly Jerry moved on to an orchestral position. Shortly after that Howard Howard, the much-respected and admired Principal Horn player for many years a member of The Metropolitan Opera Orchestra, joined us. Howard had one of the most beautiful horn sounds I could ever imagine. He brought a warmth and spectrum of color to his playing that was an inspiration. Maybe it was from working with so many magnificent singers. I will never forget his soaring tone in the Barber Summer Music. Every time I hear the piece I think of him.

In those days the Met played a summer season in Newport, Rhode Island, and Howard logically went there as part of the Met orchestra. When one of the directors of the Metropolitan Opera tour saw the historic houses, he thought what a natural place to have a chamber music festival. The first year was a very successful weekend of concerts. In its second year Howard was able to get the Lark Quintet invited to play in what was expanded into a full-week schedule. The festival became an enormous success highlighting lesser-known works written generally at the time the homes were built. After a few years Mark Malkovich, II took over the continuation of the festival. As a result of research I was doing at the Bibliothec National in Paris for a sabbatical project at The Hartt School of Music that coincided with the period of the houses. Mark cast me as the festival's resident oboe soloist. Mark was very generous and supportive of my work.

On a particularly memorable evening known as the Patron's Gala when all of the supporters of the festival were invited, I went before the concert to find my oboe in the hotel room where I was staying, only to discover it had been stolen. The concert had to be delayed for a half hour so the police could open a few of the local high schools to find me a playable oboe. The concert proceeded with my playing on a combination of two completely different oboes that sort of worked.

After the concert the Board President, of the festival, Mrs. Barbara Benjamin Cook (known as "Kittymouse," a name given to her by her father) came to me insisting that I leave the hotel and move into a large house she was living in. The house was known as "Booth Den," named after the man who built it, Edwin Booth, the brother of the John Wilkes Booth, who assassinated Lincoln. Edwin had been an internationally celebrated actor and felt he had to end his career and withdraw from the stage. He retired from performing and built his home in a town adjacent to Newport. It is a magnificent house and I was given his bedroom for almost twenty years.

Obviously Kittymouse and I became very good friends until she died. She taught me much about life. After Kittymouse died, her best friend, Lydia Foote, who was the new President of the Festival called me saying, "I guess I've inherited you!" I stayed with Lydia and we became lifelong friends. She and her daughter also Lydia who lives in Italy continued the tough job of mentoring me. To this day I remain a close friend of the whole family. And after my friend Lydia Foote passed. I was "inherited" by a cousin of Kittymouse, Lisette Prince who lives in Newport and has been a great friend and supporter in every way.

My experience at the Newport Music Festival was life altering. So much good has come from my time there and the genuine friends who I met as a result of being there.

Another important influence in my musical life was the Music Mountain Festival in Falls Village, Connecticut where I have played many summers and have conducted a series of oboe master classes for nineteen years. Its director Nicholas Gordon kept that festival going with a dedication and determination that are legendary, has recently retired. Nickolas takes great pride in noting that The Music Mountain Festival is the oldest continuous summer chamber music festival in the United States. I might add, in no small part to Nick's stubbornness.

It is amazing to me at this time of my life in music I've been invited to teach in festivals that are an important part of the future of music. The Yale Summer Chamber Music Festival in Norfolk, Connecticut and the Bowdoin International Music Festival in Brunswick, Maine and Xi'an, China are among those that remind me of the vitality and energy that young players bring to the future of classical music. These players will never let classical music end. Forget it!

I have learned from experience that playing chamber music is very difficult, because you must work hard on playing together and you must listen intently; but, at the same time, everyone around you affects your playing. It's the unspoken element. So, sometimes, making music collaboratively is a little easier. Not everything has to come from you.

Sam Baron was a wonderful and influential musician, a flute player who lived here in New York. He was the flutist of the Bach Aria Group for a number of years, and a founder of the New York Woodwind Quintet, for which Samuel Barber, Ezra Laderman, William Bergsma, Wallingford Riegger and Gunther Schuller all wrote music. Once Sam said, "The thing I love the most about chamber music is that my colleagues make me play better than I think I can play." That is such a wonderful statement and so true that your colleagues support you. They are the wind under your wings. They help you fly. Oh, what a dream. Hearing superb and dedicated artists come together to play chamber music is like a dream. They all bring to the occasion both their own personalities and all their talents for listening to one another and being inspired.

I love playing with Tom Hrynkiv, the pianist with whom I have done so much performing and recording, because I can leap into the air, and, wherever I come down, he will be there to catch me.

John Wion, whom I mentioned to you earlier was the flutist with the New York City Opera for many years and with whom I played in the Lark Woodwind Quintet, said to me once, "My ideal chamber-music experience would be to read a piece and hear everything that happens without the need to discuss anything. You just listen and play." I could not agree with him more. That has also become my own ideal.

Can you tell me more about your long experience with the Bach Aria Group? What did you learn playing with them?

Well, it was an interesting relationship that endured for six or seven years. Most of that time, Bloom and I played arias together. I played second oboe to him in their New York City concerts. Many of Bach's arias are scored for two oboes and some for three. I also played in the orchestra for the chorales and the sinfonias.

We began by playing at Town Hall, when it was still a primary venue for classical concerts. Then we moved to Alice Tully Hall. One year, I played first oboe in Mr. Bloom's place, because he had suffered a heart attack. He called me from the hospital to tell me what had happened, and asked me to play in his place for the Bach Aria Group tour that was to begin the following week. It was a grim and difficult situation. Of course, I canceled all that I had scheduled and went on the tour. It's fun, Bloom once said to a friend who told me, the reason he asked me to play was because I knew how to play standing.

With the Bach Aria Group I had the opportunity to work with artists whom I idolized, such singers as Maureen Forrester,[72] Eileen Farrell, Benita Valente, and Lois Marshall,[73] the magnificent violinist Oscar Shumsky,[74] as well as flutists Sam Baron and Julius Baker.[75] The cellist was Bernard Greenhouse.[76] All great musicians.

The tour, of about fourteen concerts, began in Toronto. After the first concert there, Oscar Shumsky introduced me to Glenn Gould, as they were very good friends. I had a unique opportunity of having a conversation with Mr. Gould. He said to me, "If I played oboe, I would like to play the way you do." I laughed and said, "That's because in my early years of studying, just after you recorded the Goldberg Variations in 1955, I bought the recording and listened to it two or three times a day. I got your phrasing in my bones." He laughed and said, "You sure did." What an incredible honor it was for me that he felt that way!

During the last week of the tour I took each musician to lunch separately, to show my appreciation for their individual support and kindnesses to me. They helped me believe that I was up to this job that was so suddenly thrust upon me. I also asked for suggestions about improving my performance. I wanted to continue to grow and learn.

---

72   Maureen Forrester (1930-2010): Canadian contralto.

73   Lois Marshall (1924-1997): Canadian soprano.

74   Oscar Shumsky (1917-2000): American violinist and conductor.

75   Julius Baker (1915-2003): American flute player, who played with the New York Philharmonic for 18 years.

76   Bernard Greenhouse (1916-2011): American cellist and one of the founding members of the Beaux Arts Trio.

Everyone had unique and helpful comments. Oscar Shumsky suggested I learn to play on the oboe some violin etudes that had meant a lot to him. Sam Baron recommended studying the music in great detail, singing every part, the bass line, the inner harmony, everything.

Bernard Greenhouse was most influential; he truly changed my life. He said that my playing was too extroverted. I was going to the audience too much, which meant to him that I didn't trust my own internal ability. Bernie told me a great story about being with Casals. He told me that while he was a student of Casals he was helping the Maestro on tour in South America with the logistical details of the performances. One concert in particular, Casals was playing in a Soccer stadium of several thousand seats and Bernie asked Casals if they would need to provide amplification? Casals said to him, "No, No, I will play so softly they will have to listen!" Genius! Bernie helped me to go more inside as I played. He said, "Bring the audience onstage. Don't go to the audience all the time." He even helped me to put this concept into practice during performances. We did experiments of this concept during actual performances. He told me to start playing an aria, as I usually did, in the middle of the auditorium and focus on slowly bringing the audience onstage to be with us in a more intimate setting. This changed my playing and my whole life entirely.

Before making this change in my performance, I had never received a bad review. Critics had given me wonderful reviews—I was this great media star American oboe star and blah, blah, blah. My new, internalized playing confused the critics. They failed to understand I was heading into new territory. They occasionally said things about me that was not so complimentary, but I believed in what I was doing.

I recall vividly my first negative review commented on the fact that, "I was not perfect." The comments weren't all bad but the critic said just enough to hurt, and it broke my heart. I was so disappointed that I called my completely supportive manager at the time, Vincent Wagner. Vincent wisely said to me, "Listen, you're in very good company. Some of the greatest artists have received reviews that are not always positive. Don't worry about it. Now you're finally becoming a grownup." I felt much better after that.

Critics saying things about you that are not always nice or even sometimes painful and seeing those words in print is even more difficult. Oscar Wilde is reported to have said that critics are the people who walk onto a battlefield after the battle is over and shoot the wounded. Certainly, onstage you put your heart out in front, so the audience can see you—and your vulnerability—and all the work you have done to get on to that platform. If they reject you, it hurts. If they are mean or off-handed it hurts, but I understand it sells newspapers and it is necessary for critics to say what they believe. I'll survive; the sun will come up the next morning.

Chapter 11. Personal

Austin High School Orchestra, Maywood, Illinois, 1954

Relaxing at home 1976

Daniel Pereira: *Bert, could we travel all the way back to the beginning of your life in music? How did you come to play the oboe?*

Humbert Lucarelli: Yes, it's an unusual story. When I was young, long before I had been introduced to the oboe, I played baseball. In Little League I was a pitcher—and a pretty good one. I really enjoyed pitching, especially the psychology of the performance and its intensity. It appealed to me because pitchers are "on" the whole time they're in the game. My pitching capabilities were similar to my later talents as an oboist. I was good at controlling location. I could place the ball pretty much at any point in the strike zone where an individual batter was weak. At fourteen, my pitching record for my age group was one of the best in the state of Illinois. So a future in professional baseball seemed real for me. A scout for the Chicago White Sox had approached my Dad about the possibility of my going to a summer baseball camp.

On the evening of October 21, at the age of fourteen, walking home from practice, there was someone in the street whose car had stalled just across the street from the house where we lived on Homan Avenue. I decided to help him push his car to the gas station, a half block away. Because it was growing dark—and the taillights were out—another vehicle did not see us and rear-ended the car that I was pushing with me caught in between. My legs were almost completely severed. My mom said she heard the screaming and knew it was me. They called her from the hospital.

I underwent a twelve-hour surgery to save my legs—to put them back together remaining in traction for three months—and was unable to walk comfortably for nearly a year and a half. My father, being concerned about my future, since baseball seemed no longer be an option, said to me, "You're going to high school soon; you've got to do something." I said, "What do you want me to do?" He said, "Why don't you play the oboe? It's my favorite instrument." He recalled the oboe from his childhood; it was a folk instrument that he had heard shepherds playing in the fields in Italy. They called it a *bifara*.[77] Anyway, I said to him, "What's an oboe?" And he said, "Oh, you're so smart. Go find out."

The next day, at my high school, I went to the band room and asked the band director for an oboe. I still remember the moment that I opened the case; the feel of the instrument, and the smell like stale, rancid saliva. It's very strange and at the same time, a well-known odor to wind players. It was unforgettable; it was as if something magical had happened. In that moment I knew that my whole life had changed. So I started playing the oboe.

Honestly, I think this experience of having to recover from that accident and learning to walk (an activity that we all think is natural and assumed was normal and easy) is what made me know I could learn to play the oboe and become a musician. If I could learn to walk after what I had been through, then I could learn anything.

Because I had good training from the very beginning, I developed a mature sound very early. There was a clarinet teacher at my high school (Austin High School), who had written a book about clarinet playing. I asked him to autograph it and he wrote, "To the young man with the beautiful sound." I still have it and can show it to you.

My first oboe teacher while I was at Austin was Robert Mayer,[78] who was the English horn player for The Chicago Symphony Orchestra. So, from the outset, I was lucky to have had exceptional training. Working with Mayer and having good guidance from him was critical to my future. In fact, he started many young players on their path to major careers.

In high school, I progressed rapidly. My best friend at that time, who helped start me on the oboe, was Richard Kantor, who was one year ahead of me also studying with Mr. Mayer. After high school Dick went on to study with Marcel Tabuteau, who I have mentioned before, the world-famous oboe teacher at The Curtis Institute and principal oboist of the Philadelphia Orchestra.

It never occurred to me that I could go to the Curtis Institute and study with Mr. Tabuteau. At the time, I did not have the confidence to apply for his class or at Juilliard. I later found out, had I applied to Juilliard I would have been granted a full scholarship because they did not have any oboe students. They were hiring outside professional freelance oboe players in New York for their orchestra concerts.

After high school I went instead to the University of Illinois in Champaign, Urbana. My year at the University of Illinois was a disaster. I was suddenly

---

77 Bifara: an Italian double-reed folk instrument.

78 Robert Mayer (1910–1994), American oboist and English horn player, who performed with the Chicago Symphony from 1931–1956.

thrust into the competitive environment where there were other fine players. For the first time, I heard other oboists my age playing very well and even, in some cases, better than me. It terrified me. Having come from an insular immigrant family, I was young, naïve and trying to succeed in this big and important school. It was a dark time. I developed an intractable case of what I call "freshman-itis." I became very negative and lost touch with the big picture; my dream.

It reached such a crisis point that, every time I touched the instrument even if it was in the case, I spiked a fever of 104 degrees, not being able to play at all. I believed it was psychosomatic, and so went to a therapist who changed my way of thinking. He cleverly avoided the whole issue of psychoanalysis, of trying to make me understand the complexity of who I was. Instead, he said to me, "There is an easy solution. Stop playing the oboe." I said, "How am I going to stop playing the oboe? That's not possible." The oboe is everything to me." It was my path into the future. I was in love with it. He said, "Then stop what you are doing." I returned to Chicago and met Ray Still who had just come to The Chicago Symphony Orchestra and began studying with him.

On a different subject now, when did you arrive in New York City from Chicago?

I went to New York in the early 1960s. To be exact, on New Year's Day, 1961. I was twenty-five years old.

What did you discover about living in New York City that was different from living in Chicago, your hometown?

Chicago is a truly creative great city. So much in the arts and commerce has emerged from Chicago. I love Chicago. It is a remarkable city! The architecture alone is stunning and The Chicago Symphony was, and still is, one of the world's greatest orchestras. But at that time in Chicago you were either "in," or you were "out." In Chicago, I was "in." I played in The Lyric Opera, Grant Park and had all the other freelance work available, from record dates to ad hoc concerts all over the city. I didn't necessarily enjoy being "in." I needed to create my own environment. Although, I, like most people, wanted to be accepted. I was never comfortable being an "in" person because it made me feel "owned."

In New York I found many different "ins" and many different "outs"—so many creative individuals doing so many things. I could get involved in contemporary music, I could just play classical chamber music, or I could work in orchestras or even in commercial music, or chamber music. Knowing that I wasn't compelled to travel down just one avenue was important for me. It blew me away completely because I was so accustomed to the idea that, if you belonged to the Chicago Symphony or you studied with someone from the Chicago Symphony, then you were "accepted." In New York, it wasn't that way, not at all. It was much more open and varied.

I also discovered, of course, that New York was not waiting for me. I had to muster the courage to survive. In my first year in New York, I earned $300. Three or four years passed before I was making enough money to eat.

Fortunately, I arrived with savings. I even had a car, but ultimately I had to sell it, in order to eat and pay my rent. My beloved little orange Volkswagen, my Beetle, my treasured orange Beetle, I had to sell it.

My rule was to make my living only from music. I determined that working in a nondescript job to support myself was unacceptable. If I couldn't make my living from music I was going to get out. I was stubborn. If the oboe and music were going to be my life, then I had to be single-minded. In the end I had to believe in myself.

So I stuck with it. I was finally able to earn a living playing in orchestras, doing chamber music or solos. It didn't matter, as long as I played the oboe anywhere. That's all that was important.

So, that's what you really wanted, above everything else?

I was lucky to be able to know that money coming in was a byproduct of my love for making music. Of course, I had to be aware of whether I had five cents or fifty dollars in my pocket. Still, I didn't do things just for the money, not really. At least, I hope not.

Corollary to your last comment, the life of a musician is difficult and living with a musician is likewise difficult, because throughout our entire careers, we musicians devote so much time to practice. By necessity we must focus time and attention on ourselves; our technique, our talent, and our intellectual growth. Has such intense focus adversely affected your private life?

I have surrounded myself with people who understand and have allowed me to put my immersion in music first. The people who inhabit my life understand it, appreciate it and enjoy it. And put up with me.

I often had to make painful choices, including being unable to attend my father's funeral. That was a difficult time for me. I was often absent from Christmas Eve dinners; away from my family at holidays because I was playing concerts, and my family sacrificed for me. My making the choice, but it seems there was no choice.

Ray Still said it plainly: "Being an oboe player is a long, murky road."

Beyond the classical music world, what style of music do you like? When you are home or while you are driving, do you listen to pop, rock or jazz?

I am not a big fan of jazz. Most of the jazz I hear seems sort of introverted. It's for itself or for the person who is playing, not necessarily for the audience. I suppose some classical musicians are the same. A lot of that music feels to me a little like going to a party to which I have not been invited. Of course, that is a very personal perception and I know is flawed. I'm finally beginning to change.

Some of my jazz player friends say to me, "How can you play the same notes all the time". It's hard for them to understand I play the same notes all the time differently.

On the other hand, we need to understand each other and that every performer—and every performance—is unique, and some do absolutely incredible things. But I have to confess some music just doesn't appeal to me, like heavy metal or, what I jokingly call, "Park Avenue folk music." I am too emotional. If I'm relaxing I like popular music, simple ballads and love songs. I am a sucker for a good love song.

I enjoy listening to Barbra Streisand.

Oh, so do I. Barbra Streisand. She is a fascinating mix of craft, emotion and struggle in the act of performing. I have heard that she suffers from severe stage fright. The nerves may come from the necessity of living up to her recordings. She is also famous for her perfectionism. I am sure she could never just let that aspect of her character go. She is so intense. She knows what she was doing; she knows the craft, like Sinatra, who also had the craft. There are so many popular singers who are accomplished musicians and provide a genuine model. They just sound natural. It takes a lot of work to just sound natural.

For a while in New York I enjoyed playing backup on recordings with popular singers, and did some crossover solo recordings of my own like *The Sensual Sound of the Soulful Oboe.* For me, that recording flowed. It was an important recording in my life because the producer Joe Abend, who was brilliant at marketing, became a close personal friend. He was a great human being. That recording is probably still the best selling oboe record in history.

Some people became jealous of my career and I even got death threatening letters and phone calls. Two letters were cut outs of words from magazines and newspapers saying things like. "Who do you think you are trying to be a big shot soloist?"

Jealousy is probably the stupidest emotion of all. I used to be jealous when I was young, in my mid-twenties and had a great conversation about it with Dick Perlman who was an assistant to the Franco Zeffirelli the great opera and film director. Dick, in fact, went on to become the Director of the opera program at the Eastman School of Music. Anyway, we were taking one time about my jealousy and he said to me, "What a stupid attitude. It only means you want what someone else has without the work and sacrifice and responsibility they have to endure. If you want something just get up off you butt and go get it and endure all they have had to." That conversation changed my life. I never want what someone else has. I have learned find out what I want and go get it.

People thought I had become financially independent. Not true, *The Sensual Sound* was my first recording of that sort with the producer Joe Abend, and I was paid per session. I still had to worry about how I was going to get to my next gig, by bus, subway or walking. Joe got me to do several other "crossover" recordings that he made commercially successful. Most of it was like the slow movements of oboe concertos having qualities that are similar to ballads. One of my personal favorite recordings was one I did with harpist Susan Jolles of the music of Debussy, and another with Frank Morelli, also with Susan, of mixed impressionistic and romantic French music.

You have quite an active life as a teacher and, until a few years ago, as a performer as well. But I imagine you like to rest from time to time. What is your ideal vacation? What do you like to do in your down time?

The most restful vacations I have ever had were in the Caribbean. In the Caribbean, I have nothing to do but sit in the sun and drink margaritas. I like to rent a place with a kitchen, where I can do my own cooking. The first day is a big workday, doing all of my shopping and cooking for the entire week. After that, I just read and sit in the sun.

Having nothing to do is rare in my life. Even at home I am invariably busy. Having nothing to do can be a good thing but I can't do *nothing* for too long; one week, maximum ten days.

I also love just being with friends who I rarely otherwise see and who have unusual ideas; ideas unlike my own.

Do you ever get bored at all?

Do I ever get bored? No, no. That would be bizarre. Such interesting things always happening, so many interesting people and ideas in the world. And my own head is filled with activity. I am always preoccupied with making things better; improving. There is no time to be bored.

At this point in our conversation I would like to enter the realm of religion and faith. Can you talk about your spiritual or religious beliefs?

I was raised Roman Catholic. I was even an altar boy. My sister and I suspect that my grandmother on my father's side was Jewish. For my sister's confirmation in the Catholic Church my grandfather, who worked for the Stark Piano Company in Chicago took some scraps of ebony to a member of our family who made jewelry and asked him to design a cross for her with little silver tips. But, in accordance with his wishes, in the middle of the cross was placed a Star of David. I remember my grandfather saying to my sister: "I never want you to forget who you are." Even though I was an alter boy at The Church of Mother Cabrini in Chicago, I used to go to Synagogue often on Saturdays. My wise father said he did not want me to be afraid of what others were doing behind their doors of worship.

Although I identify as a Catholic, I am not at this time actively practicing. For me, all churches are simultaneously great and flawed. They are like people, because people made them. They have all the vices and the virtues of human beings.

I feel no particular need to engage in any routine religious practice. Perhaps as years pass and I am closer to acknowledging my mortality, like so many people, I will renew my religious faith. At the moment I don't know and I don't need to know about life after death or even if a God exists. Just a month before he died, my father jokingly said to me, "I'm going to find out what's going on here before you do."

Many Italians have a loose, quixotic relationship with the Church. I respect any devout person who attends church regularly, like my sister. One Christmas I went back to Chicago to visit and she took me to midnight mass. It was quite a show with guitars and people singing like pop singers, but it didn't feel like I was attending a mass. It was more of a commercial event; a show. I had no patience for it. It was not my idea of a religious service. My sister asked for my opinion and, not wanting to judge, I said, "It's charming." About four days later, after I returned home to New York, she called me. Her first words were, "Charming my foot."

I prefer the old ways: The Latin mass and liturgical music that is older. Religions these days are trying to be relevant—to be appealing—and so do classical music and musicians. I think every time you do something to be more popular you offend as many people as you attract. We are afraid of being who and what we are. One of the nicest things I ever heard anybody say about the Vatican was many years ago, came from Bryant Gumbel on *The Today Show*. He said that the Vatican was keeping history alive. Symphony orchestras and concerts of classical music do likewise. Classical musicians devote themselves to music and to the premise that a spiritual connection can be accessed through the artistic experience. We keep the history of that experience alive. I take pride in that.

Museums and orchestras need not be current or relevant. They are. They can just be what they are and trust that their presence; as they exist is sufficient. Perhaps I am naïve for believing this. In New York, we have the Museum of Modern Art, the Whitney and the Metropolitan. Different museums serve different purposes. I once asked a musicologist what his field was, his area of specialization?" He said, "Twentieth-century musicology." I thought to myself, "Twentieth century? Why does the twentieth-century need a musicologist? We're living it." But he is right; contemporary music scholars are needed. It is an important part of our history.

I have a general question for you. What has music taught you as a person, as a human being? Do you think you have become a better or a different person because you are a musician?

Oh, of course. Music has forced me to confront myself, to understand my weaknesses and my strengths, my foolishness, and my stupidity. It goes even deeper than psychoanalysis but is much more fun than psychoanalysis. Certainly I have suffered pain in my journey as a musician, but I have loved doing what I do. I am lucky to have grown to appreciate the love of ideas; this is the reason people can grow old with vitality. Every person I know over 100 cares more about ideas than about themselves.

Do you know many people over 100?

So far, I have known about eight or ten—a lot. It is amazing, humbling and it is a privilege. Every one of them has embraced the quality of caring more about others and about ideas than they do about themselves. I also see in them certainly some narcissism. We wouldn't be human otherwise. If I recall correctly, Freud said being narcissistic is human. It seems an awkward contradiction; but so is life.

A few days ago, I noticed a couple traveling on a bus. I would not say that they were ugly, but they were certainly not conventionally attractive. They were looking at one another like they were looking at gold. They were in heaven. It almost made me cry because I thought, "Oh, there is a God. God put these two people together." It is so mystical and made them beautiful. In the end, I know that about myself; that some people make me feel beautiful—that was my family—and some don't. As I have told you, my grandmother said to me, "Always surround yourself with people who make you believe you are more than you think you are."

Let's now free-fall through some of the friends who have had an important impact on your life.

You had the opportunity to meet the famous Russian ballet and modern dancer Rudolf Nureyev,[79] who, sadly, died prematurely in 1993 at age fifty-five. What do you remember about your encounter with Nureyev?

As everyone says, he was an athletic performer. He could leap into the air and just hover; just incredible. He was also famously temperamental. We met by chance. I was in New Orleans performing as principal oboist of the Royal Ballet of London and a friend of mine, who was hosting a party, sent a Rolls Royce limousine to pick me up backstage after the concert and go the party. I walked out of the stage door, and Nureyev, who had just performed Romeo in Prokofiev's Romeo and Juliet with Margo Fonteyn[80] and the Royal Ballet, was behind me. He headed toward the Rolls because after all he was the star; he thought it was his. I said to him, "Rudy, no, no, no, this is mine. Can I give you a lift to the party?" So, we rode together to the party.

That's how you met?

Yes that was our first meeting. He just laughed and went into hysterics. And then we talked in the limousine. I saw him again socially on several occasions. In fact, after a while—this was during a period when playing with The Royal Ballet— when I routinely stayed out late after the performances, because you are filled with adrenaline after a performance. I went to bars with friends and fellow musicians, returning to the hotel in the early morning hours. He always waited for me in the hotel lobby. He read a newspaper until I arrived. He wanted to make sure that I was okay. Although he had a reputation of being very severe, he was always very kind and generous with me. I had no more of a relationship with him than that except at one point, when I got sick, he put me in touch with Doctor Rolf Vang, his doctor in New York who had been, as a young man, an assistant to Albert Schweitzer[81]

---

79 Rudolf Nureyev (1938-1993): Soviet-born dancer of ballet and modern dance.

80 Dame Margo Fonteyn de Arias (1919–1991), English ballerina.

81 Albert Schweitzer (1875–1965), German-born theologian, organist, philosopher, physician and medical missionary in Africa.

in Africa. Rolf and I became close friends, because there was a magical quality and depth about his personality that I found completely engrossing.

You were a close friend to Brian McDonnell.[82] How did your relationship with him affect your life?

I saw the freedom with which Brian approached living, without fear. He was fearless in the navigation of both his personal life and his public life. Brian was raised Catholic and almost ordained as a Jesuit. They are most creative, these Jesuits! They have such complete minds for reasoning, understanding and doubting as well as accepting. Fantastic way of thinking!

Brian was for a time involved in the Federal Government's drug rehabilitation program. He told me about a meeting at the White House, where they were discussing America's drug abuse problem, one of the members of the White House staff made the claim that there were no drugs near the White House. Brian responded, "Oh, really?" The meeting was about to break for lunch, so he just said, "Okay, I'll see you guys after lunch." Then he went outside and, within a couple of blocks of the White House, bought all kinds of drugs; cocaine, heroin, marijuana. After lunch he returned with his bag of newly acquired toys. He emptied the bag on a table and said to the gathering: "Gentlemen, I just bought these within three blocks of this room."

Brian had enormous personal power. It is amazing that he could go three blocks from the White House to buy heroin. He could look anybody in the eye and know. And I'm embarrassed to tell you similar experiences of that sort myself. Brian inspired me to be open to what others were seeing, saying, thinking and feeling, and not to judge. My father also taught me this. My father never condemned anyone for being what or who he or she was. His acceptance was complete, totally embracing.

When my father died in 1990, I didn't attend his funeral because I was teaching in Vancouver. My sister helped me make the difficult decision not to go. She said, "Daddy would prefer that you just do what you are doing; teaching. Come if you want to, for yourself. Don't come to make a show for the relatives." So I didn't go. I stayed in Vancouver and did my job. Months later I gave my father a memorial service in New York. Over 100 people attended, a lot of New Yorkers who had met my father attended. It was a bizarre collection of characters, a cross-section of the City, so wildly disparate. These people all felt the same about him, that he wholly accepted them as unique individuals.

I try to emulate my father. I try not to judge. At concerts by colleagues—oboists especially—I don't judge, because I love hearing them play. I learn from them all, even characteristics that I want to avoid. I don't judge while I'm listening.

Being a competition juror is difficult for me. In that setting, I have a responsibility to separate players from one another. In a concert, listeners

82 John Brian McDonnell (1943–2003), born in Scranton, Pennsylvania, was a former Jesuit seminarian and became an anti-war activist and social worker.

just want to enjoy themselves. They don't go to judge; at least I don't. Most of the people I know don't. They pay money to have a good time, no matter the details of your playing. Listeners go after the good part of you. You're giving them a party. You can't give a bad party because everybody wants to have a good time. Concerts are a party.

When Brian McDonnell went on a hunger strike at Lafayette Square in Washington, D.C., you decided to go there and play for him.

Yes. I had just recently met him, but immediately I saw in him something touching and powerful. It was a time for me when I was even thinking about doing things that were more socially relevant, like starting a soup kitchen. Brian's hunger strike was to protest our entry into Cambodia. He did not eat for approximately forty-five days, and nearly died. I played the oboe for him in the park. While I was there playing, someone from the White House came to the Square and told Brian that Henry Kissinger would like to meet with him. He agreed. They sent a limousine and Brian invited me to go along.

We were driven to a farm in Maryland. Kissinger was there, along with the journalist Sander Vanocur.[83] Kissinger's task was to persuade Brian to eat and go off the strike. The pivotal moment came when Kissinger said to him, "Brian, I agree with you. We should not be in Cambodia. But your dying will not stop the conflict. It will only remove your influence from the debate." This resonated with Brian. He promised Kissinger that he would stop his hunger strike and he did.

On the drive back to Washington, we passed a Baskin-Robbins ice cream parlor. Brian asked the driver to stop. Giving me some money, he said, "Go in there and get me a banana split." I said, "A banana split? Are you crazy? Three scoops of ice cream, a banana, and chocolate with whipped cream? That will kill you. You haven't eaten for over a month and a half." He said, "Get me a banana split. I've been dreaming about a banana split for six weeks." I got him his banana split. He ate it all, and he was fine. He survived the hunger strike—and the banana split.

Thank you for sharing this story with me.

Brian was a magical person. He understood the power of the mind over the body. His wife, Alice, also became a good friend of mine. An African-American, she dedicated her life to working inside prisons, rehabilitating convicted felons; some very dangerous men. Walking home one evening after work, tragically, two boys mugged her. They wanted her money. It would have been typical of her to say, "What do you want? Do you need food? What do you need the money for? Come on, come home with me." They fought. She fell on a knife and was killed. I played at her funeral but broke down in mid-performance. I wept. I couldn't play. For a wind player, of course, sobbing while trying to blow air through the instrument is not

---

83 Sander Vanocur (b. 1928), American journalist national political correspondent of NBC News for the White House during the 1960s and early 1970s.

helpful at all. I have since learned to avoid this pitfall.

Alice was a beautiful person. She had an innate sense of understanding and directness. She seemed to live without shame or self-doubt. To her, the world was transparent. She saw through its complexity as if it were a piece of Plexiglas. I hope she taught me to do the same.

This gift is innate in children and audiences alike. They see right through you. But trauma compels us to put up shields for protection. We develop an opaque screen between the world and ourselves, instead of accepting it and ourselves.

Brian died before his time as well, of cancer, but he lived a full life. Both Brian and Alice were powerful and impassioned people, who affected me greatly.

Your long-time student and close friend Dr. William Frosch is a well-known psychiatrist living and working in New York. How has your friendship with him— his approach to life, to psychology, and his understanding of the brain and the mind—influenced your artistry, your performing and your life?

Yes, Dr. Frosch is important to me. I have enormous respect and admiration for him and his work. He has affected me deeply, in that, like so many good friends, he brings out the best of me.

He provokes honesty. I try to be honest not only with myself but also with my audience, and with everyone I know. The audience is an extension of my life. My listeners are my friends. Heifetz perhaps considered the audience as a kind of adversary. He played with such authority, strength and accuracy that he forced his listeners to yield.

I don't feel that so much. I hope to persuade my listeners, gently, to accept; I mean in the sense of a deep, intimate friendship. I want them to accept what I am and who I am.

Have you ever been through psychoanalysis?

As I told you I went to a therapist when I was in college, and as we talked earlier about trying to reconcile my musical and professional life, but no, no actual psychoanalysis. I thought of it once. In Dr. Frosch's company I feel so comfortable that I don't even think about myself. He promotes self-acceptance. This helps me as an artist, as a musician. I think a performer who feels accepted will open up more and give more. Maybe in personal relationships, too. You can see it in interviews that Larry King did and now Charlie Rose. The respect and acceptance they extend to a guest makes the guest feel secure and free to be open. My Newport friend Kitty-mouse used to say, with real New England wisdom, "You get more with honey than with vinegar."

This translates into teaching. With students who accept my suggestions, I feel less obliged to defend my ideas. I tell my students, when you study with someone else, the first step is to let the teacher know that they are believed. The teacher should never feel doubted or challenged. If I sense that you believe me, I can play—or teach—in a much freer and open way and give 100% of myself.

You have told me that your father was a crucial influence in your life. Can you share a little more about him? And also the degree to which your Italian heritage has influenced your approach to making music?

We talk a lot about my Dad who was such a complex influence, but we can't forget that my Mom gave me with love and acceptance, the earth I stand on.

Playing opera when I was young—for five years—had a tremendous impact on my character and on my playing. My playing lies more in the *bel canto* style. I like to sing when I play. I think I do that, because, in my early years, I heard so much singing. Again, as my grandmother said, "You become what you eat."

My father sang or whistled Puccini and Verdi arias. He knew the arias in their entirety. He even sang soprano arias. Whether he sang soprano or baritone or tenor mattered little to him.

Was he any good?

Not bad. When I was six years old, he took me to my first live staged musical performance, The Merry Widow. I was completely blown away. Seeing that stage, I still remember the scene where it was snowing on stage. The stage was all blue, the snow was coming down, and the singing was like magic. Magic. That is what we do. We make people feel the snow coming down, and the colors.

Last night, my friend Oli and I were talking about the four elements of music—you know, rhythm, pitch, dynamics, and color, which is an idea I got from *The Psychology of Music* by Carl Seashore.[84] Oli said, "What does it mean, color? In music, there is no such thing." *Mamma mia!* It was already quite late and had a lot of wine, so I said, "Oli, it would take us another bottle of wine to get through color. You must understand it, so we'll argue about color some other time." Then he teased me, and so I said in the simplest way, "A, E, I, O, U in Italian. Those are different colors." Then he knew right away, and he said, "You got me." Curious, this enormously intelligent man, but he had never conceptualized this idea before. You remember I told you once, when I play, I think vowel sounds. Music students should study phonetics.

So your father introduced you to the oboe, correct?

Yes. As a child, he went to the opera in Rome, which was about an hour away from Sora, his hometown, where he was born in the province of Frosinone. In those days he said if you bought a train ticket, you automatically got a ticket to the opera. Admission was included in the train ticket. You'd show your train ticket at the opera house and they'd let you in. Isn't that incredible?

Yes, it is.

He went often; regularly. At that time, opera-goers took food with them, sat in the balcony and ate lunch. Now, you can't bring food into a hall. I like

---

84   Carl Emil Seashore (1866–1949), American psychologist.

watching Metropolitan Opera productions in movie theaters. You can bring your popcorn and soda, sit there and watch. It's very inviting, like being at a baseball game. Over time, we have turned concert going into a rarified, petrified experience rather than a simple human one.

So, would you say that opera is still the first, number-one genre in classical music?

It depends on how you look at it. It seems to me that opera brings together so many different art forms such as music, dance and theater, including set design. In that regard, it is an all-encompassing art form that is comprehensive.

Do you believe that opera attracts more people?

I don't know if it attracts larger or smaller audiences than other genres, but it is not necessarily the number-one musical experience. I know some people who hate opera. It simply has a larger audience base. For me, the number-one musical experience is the one I am having at the moment; if it absorbs me. I am sure you know what I mean. If you are utterly taken by a performance, it could be a Schubert Lied, a Mahler song cycle, a Beethoven symphony or an opera. It absorbs you. People ask me, "Who is your favorite composer?" I can't answer that question. Whoever I am playing or listening to is my favorite composer. It doesn't matter if it is Beethoven, Britten or Bartók. It's my favorite. And I must believe that, because, if I don't, how can I make my audience believe it?

Argentinean philosopher Jorge Bucay,[85] one of my favorite writers at present, defined love as "the altruistic task of creating the necessary space to let the other person be who she or he is." Do you believe in true love? What is love for you?

Well, yes, precisely. But perhaps it is more than creating space. And maybe I would include the word conditions, to create the conditions in which the person you love can be fulfilled. That's the real goal of a relationship, if you can find someone. Again, forgive me for repeating myself, I'm becoming an old man like Strauss, my grandmother's advice comes back to me: "Surround yourself with people who help you dream of being more than you think you can be." People in my life have helped me be more than I dreamt I could ever be. I hope I can do the same for every person that I come into contact with. Forgive me, in that regard I want to help everyone.

In this case, in this case not so bad I don't think you need to be forgiven.

That may be my main mission. If I were an institution and had to write a mission statement, it would be to help create conditions—for my friends, everyone I know, people with whom I relate—that enable them to be fulfilled. Like that wonderful Bette Midler song The Wind beneath My Wings. If I can be that, why not? That would be a great mission, a great role, to be that for people whom I respect and care about. Does that come close to an answer?

---

85 Jorge Bucay (b. 1949), gestalt psychotherapist and author.

SPECIAL CITY FEATURE: FOCUS ON MONTRÉAL
SEPTEMBER 2004 US $9.50 / CANADA $11.95
GRAMOPHONE
THE CLASSICAL MUSIC MAGAZINE

BACH

'Bach by Bert'
Cantatas – Nos 12, 156, 249 – Sinfonia[a]. Oboe
Partita in G minor, BWV1013 (arr Lucarelli
from Flute Partita in A minor). Oboe Sonata
in G minor, BWV1030[b]
Humbert Lucarelli *ob* [a]Krista Bennion
Feeney, [a]Anca Nicolau *vns* [a]Ronald
Lawrence *va* [a]Myron Lutzke *vc* [a]John
Feeney *db* [ab]Bradley Brookshire *hpd*
Crystal Records Ⓟ CRYSTALCD726
(51 minutes: DDD)

**A colourful, memorable recital that boasts
a deeply expressive soloist in Lucarelli**

Bach by Bert
Oboist
Humbert Lucarelli
performs
Partita, Sonata
& Sinfonias by
J.S. Bach

Around the time I started
to play the cello, Pablo
Casals' recordings of the
Bach Suites were reissued
and I couldn't get enough
of them. Eventually, I
came to know every idio-
syncratic use of colour and
nuance, every turn of phrase. It was an education
so narrowly focused and intense that it propelled
me into music as my life's passion.

(continued from previous page.)

Humbert Lucarelli's new recital could be like that for young oboists. He has invested in every note a lifetime of thought and feeling to the extent that nothing is extraneous, everything is committed to making music. And while this may be more immediately obvious from the three sinfonias, with their seductive reflections on mortality (ironically, Lucarelli underwent bypass surgery while the recording was being finished), it is the magnificent G minor Partita that will remain in my memory, each movement with its own unforgettable personality, including a Sarabande of striking, solemn beauty.

With Adam Abeshouse's fine recording capturing to perfection Lucarelli's deeply expressive, plangent tone, this release reminds us that the music world has scant use for instrumental soloists beyond pianists, violinists and the occasional clarinettist, flautist or cellist. In an interview published in 1988, Lucarelli commented: 'Twelve concertos by [Johann Christian] Fischer. What's more colourful than a man who died during a concert while he was playing for the Queen of England? I can just see this man writing a lick for himself that was so difficult that he had a heart attack trying to play it! I think oboe players as a group are among the most colourful people in the world'.

He might have added, colourful or not, they make music fit for the gods.   **Laurence Vittes**

About Humbert Lucarelli

Photo by Lisette Prince for cover of Barber, Strauss, Wolf-Ferrari and Vaughan Williams CD, Newport, RI, 1990CD

Oboist Humbert Lucarelli has distinguished himself as one of America's foremost musicians. Hailed as "America's leading oboe recitalist" (*The New York Times*), Bert Lucarelli "has proven his preeminence among oboists today" (*The New York Daily News*) and has been cited in the *Grove's Dictionary of Music and Musicians* as one of America's well-known oboists. Mr. Lucarelli has performed and taught extensively throughout the United States, Canada, Mexico, South America, Europe, Japan, Australia and Asia. He has appeared in such music festivals as Angel Fire, Aspen, Bowdoin International Music Festival, Chautauqua, Marblehead, Martha's Vineyard, Music Mountain, Newport, Victoria International Music Festival, II Festival Eleazar de Carvalho in Brazil and the Yale School of Music Chamber Music Festival in Norfolk, Connecticut. Among his most recent engagements are master classes at the Hochschule in Cologne, at the Berlin University of the Arts and in Xi'an, China.

Mr. Lucarelli's wide range of musical activities has included performances with the American Symphony Orchestra, I Solisti Veneti, Lehigh Valley Chamber Orchestra, Orchestra of St. John's Smith Square, Orpheus Chamber Orchestra, Orquestra Sinphônica do Estado de Sâo Paulo, the Philharmonia Virtuosi as well as the Scranton Philharmonic Orchestra and Northeastern Pennsylvania Philharmonic. Concerts with the original Bach Aria Group, the Trio Bell'Arte, the American, Amernet, Audubon, Biava, Cassatt, Chester, Colorado, Emerson, Lark, Leontovich, Manhattan, Miami, Muir, Panocha, Philadelphia and Ying string quartets have brought a vast new audience to the oboe. Of his performance with I Solisti Veneti, The New York Times critic Allen Hughes wrote, "Mr. Lucarelli is a true virtuoso on the oboe."

As an orchestral performer, Mr. Lucarelli has performed and recorded under the baton of some of the world's leading conductors, including Leonard Bernstein, Arthur Fiedler, Kiril Kondrashin, Josef Krips, James Levine, Dmitri Mitropoulos, Artur Rodzinsky, Sir Georg Solti, Leopold Stokowski and Igor Stravinsky.

Mr. Lucarelli has recorded John Corigliano's Oboe Concerto for RCA Victor, which was written for and premiered by him with the American Symphony Orchestra to a standing ovation at Carnegie Hall. The numerous recordings include such labels as Koch International, Lyrichord, MCA Classics, Musical Heritage Society, Pantheon and Stradivari. Mr. Lucarelli has recorded music of Bach, Baksa, Bax, Bliss, Britten, Debussy, Hindemith, Leclair, Lefebvre, Mozart, Poulenc, Rameau, Saint-Saëns, including the oboe concerti of Strauss, Telemann, Vaughan Williams and Wolf-Ferrari. His most recent recording featuring an all-Bach program was praised in *The Gramophone* magazine as a "memorable recital that boasts a deeply expressive soloist".

Mr. Lucarelli is Professor of Oboe at The Hartt School in West Hartford, Connecticut, The Steinhardt School of Culture, Education, and Human Development at New York University, and has previously been a member of the faculty at the State University of New York at Purchase. In the summer of 2002, Bert Lucarelli was the first American oboist to be invited to perform and teach at the Central Conservatory of Music in Beijing, China.

Bert Lucarelli is the recipient of a Solo Recitalists Fellowship, Consortium Commissioning, and Music Recording grants from the National Endowment for the Arts. He has been named an Honorary Member of The International Double Reed Society.

For more information, visit www.HumbertLucarelli.com.

About Daniel Pereira

Daniel Pereira giving a lecture recital at the International Keyboard Festival & Masterclass, Tui, Spain – 2015
Photo Credit: Gus Abreu

A native of Spain, where he began his musical studies and received the Special Prize in Piano Performance, Daniel Pereira holds a Doctor of Musical Arts degree from the University of Maryland, a Master of Music degree from the University of Hartford and an Artist Diploma from the State University of New York at Purchase. While at Hartford, he was awarded the prestigious Moses Haltzmark and Hartt Alumni awards. He is also a two-time recipient of the Evelyn B. Storrs Scholarship. His doctoral thesis consisted of the live recording, in two recitals, of the complete preludes (90) of Alexander Scriabin.

Dr. Pereira participated in piano festivals and master classes in Spain, Portugal, France, Italy, Belgium, Switzerland, the Czech Republic, Brazil and the United States. He founded the Piano Friends Society of Galicia, in Spain, and was the artistic director of the International Piano Festivals

"Conde de Gondomar" held from 2000–2006 in Spain, where he also participated as a performer and lecturer. He was also co-director of the "Vianden International Music Festival" in Luxembourg. Dr. Pereira has appeared on television and radio shows, both in the U.S. and Spain and is a guest professor at the Turtle Bay Music School in New York City. He performs and lectures regularly in the U.S, Brazil and Spain, including the International Keyboard Festival & Masterclass in Tui (IKFEM).

Dr. Pereira was Director of Music at the Opus School of Music and Conservatory in the Washington D.C. He has conducted extensive research on pianists of the past, old and new recordings, and schools of piano playing at the one-of-a-kind International Piano Archives at Maryland (IPAM). He believes that this experience has greatly enriched him as a musician and pedagogue. This work has led him to create www.pianouniverse.org, a web resource for piano genealogies and traditions.

TXT9

Humbert Lucarelli's Complete Solo Discography

Bach by Bert, Partita, Sonata and Sinfonias by J. S. Bach. Crystal Records, CD726.

Premiere of Ned Rorem's *An Oboe book. Nine Pieces for Oboe and Piano*, written for Bert Lucarelli and Delores Stevens. Albany Records.

Telemann's Oboe, The Six Partitas. Well-Tempered Productions, WTP 5169, re-issue of 1968 recording for the Musical Heritage Society.

The Sounds of Remembered Dreams, Music of the fin-de-siécle for Oboe, Bassoon and Harp. Vox Classics, Vox 7504.

American Music for Oboe and Strings, Music by Barlow, Bloom, Corigliano and Wilder. Koch International 3-7187-2.

Sensazione II per Oboe Solista e Alcuni Strumenti (1983) Opus One 160 for Solo Oboe, by Larry Singer with The Hartt Contemporary Players.

Music of Steven Gryc, Opus One 166.

Oboe Concertos of Barber, Strauss, Wolf-Ferrari and Vaughan-Williams. Koch International 2-7023-4.

O'Baroque, Concerti by Albinoni, Handel and Telemann. MCA Classics MCAD-6042.

The Bel Canto Oboe. Price-less D21062.

Debussy: Music for Oboe and Harp. Stradivari Classics SCD-6034.

Pop Goes the Oboe. The Special Music Company SMC-6034.

Robert Baska Quintet for Oboe and Strings (1972). Musical Heritage Society MHS 48957.

The Sensual Sound of the Soulful Oboe. The Special Music Company SMC 4527.

Two English Oboe Quintets (Bax and Bliss). Musical Heritage Society MHS 3521.

Oboe Sonatas of Hindemith, Poulenc and Saint-Saëns. Lyrichord Discs LLST 7320.

French Baroque Trio Sonatas (Philador, Leclair and Rameau). Pantheon-FSM 63906-PAN.

Concerto for Oboe, John Corigliano. RCA/BMG Classics 60395-2-RG.

Telemann Partitas Complete (two-disc set). Musical Heritage Society MHS 996, 997.

Serenade No. 10 in Bb Major, K. 361, Wolfgang Amadeus Mozart. Musical Heritage Society MHS 855.

Benjamin Britten, Six Metamorphoses after Ovid, Op. 49, and Phantasy Quartet, Op. 2. Lyrichord Discs Inc. LLST-7195.

www.HumbertLucarelli.com

50 Performances To Remember

This selection of performances roughly shows the immense, infinite array of possibilities of the incredible artists that have been recorded on any format. I hope this short list inspires and encourages you to explore into the countless performances of the most genuine artists that God has sent down to Earth.

Enjoy.

—Daniel Pereira

Elizabeth Schwarzkopf
Morgen
by Richard Strauss
Cecilia Bartoli
Agitata da due venti
by Antonio Vivaldi
Carlos Kleiber
Symphony No. 36 "Linz"
by Wolfgang Amadeus Mozart
and anything else
Natalie Dessay
"Glitter and Be Gay" from *Candide*
by Leonard Bernstein
Bruno Walter
"Kyrie" from *Requiem* in D Minor, K.626
by Wolfgang Amadeus Mozart
Christa Ludwig
"Erbarme dich"
    from *St. Matthew Passion*, BWV 244
by Johann Sebastian Bach
Bidu Sayao
"Cantilena"
    from *Bachianas Brasileiras No. 5*
by Heitor Villa-Lobos
Vladimir Horowitz
Keyboard Sonatas
by Domenico Scarlatti
Mirella Freni
Madame Butterfly
by Giacomo Puccini
Jascha Heifetz
Violin Concerto in D Major, Op. 35
by Piotr Ilyich Tchaikovsky

Pablo Casals
Cello Suites
by Johann Sebastian Bach
Guiomar Novaes
Songs without Words
by Felix Mendelssohn
Leonard Bersntein
Symphonies
by Gustav Mahler
Dietrich Fischer-Dieskau
Lieder Cycles
by Franz Schubert
Dinu Lipatti
Impromptu in Gb Major, D. 899, No. 3
by Franz Schubert
Andres Segovia
Demonstrates different timbres of the
    guitar
An dres Segovia
Variations sur un thème de Mozart
by Segovia - Sor
Maria Callas
Anything during the 1950s
Herbert von Karajan
Missa Solemnis
by Ludwig van Beethoven
and almost anything else
David Oistrakh
Violin Concerto in D Major, Op. 61
by Ludwig van Beethoven

Alfredo Kraus
"Je crois entende" from *Les Pêcheurs des perles*
by Georges Bizet

Kathleen Battle
"Ach, Ich fuhls" from *Die Zauberflöte*, K. 620
by Wolfgang Amadeus Mozart

Claudio Arrau
Piano Concertos Nos. 1 and 2
by Johannses Brahms

Clifford Curzon
Piano Sonata No. 3 in F Minor, Op. 5
by Johannes Brahms

Placido Domingo
"E lucevan le stele" from *Tosca*
by Giacomo Puccini

Rosa Ponselle
"Casta diva" from *Norma*
by Vincenzo Bellini

Humbert Lucarelli
Canzonetta for Oboe and Strings
by Samuel Barber

Enrico Caruso
"Una furtiva lagrima" from *L'elisir d'amore*
by Gaetano Donizetti

Art Tatum
Piano solos and improvisations

Wynton Marsalis
Trumpet Concertos
by Franz Joseph Haydn

Sergiu Celibidache
Symphonies by Anton Bruckner

Wilhelm Furtwangler
"Prelude" to *Lohengrin*
by Richard Wagner

Vladimir Sofronitzky
Preludes and Sonatas for piano
by Alexander Scriabin

Victoria de los Angeles
La Traviata
by Giuseppe Verdi

Isaac Stern
Violin Concerto, Op. 77
by Johannes Brahms

Emil Gilels
Sonatas for piano
by Ludwig van Beethoven

Pablo de Sarasate
Zigeunerweizen
by Pablo de Sarasate

Arturo Toscanini
La forza del destino
by Giuseppe Verdi

Sergei Rachmaninov
Piano Concertos
by Sergei Rachmaninov

Edwin Fischer
The Well-Tempered Clavier
by Johann Sebastian Bach

Edith Piaf
French chanson

Nat King Cole
Anything!

John Coltrane/Johnny Hartman
They Say It's Wonderful

Joan Sutherland
I Puritani
by Vincenzo Bellini

Kirsten Flagstad
Wagner operas

Alicia de Larrocha
Piano pieces
by Isaac Albéniz and Enrique Granados

Carlos Gardel
Tangos

Gyorgy Sebok
Adagio from BWV 564
by Bach-Busoni

Georges Petre
Vienna's New Year's Concert 2010

Luciano Pavarotti
"Nessun dorma" from *Turandot*
by Giacomo Puccini

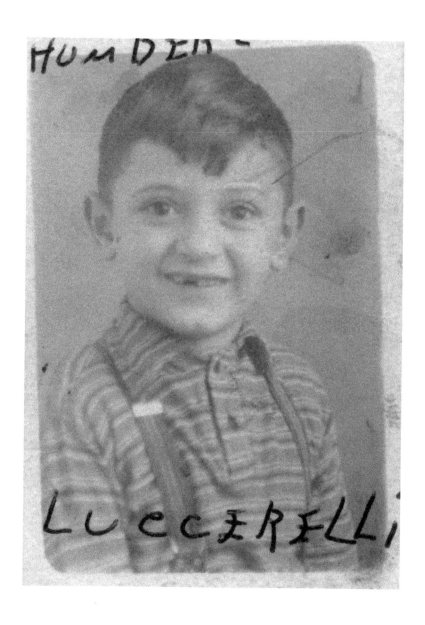